NPCA National Park Guide Series

NATIONAL PARKS AND CONSERVATION ASSOCIATION

GUIDE TO NATIONAL PARKS
NORTHEAST REGION

Written and compiled by Russell D. Butcher for the National Parks and Conservation Association and edited by Lynn P. Whitaker

NPCA is America's only private, nonprofit citizen organization dedicated solely to protecting, preserving, and enhancing the U.S. National Park System. The association's mission is to protect and enhance America's National Park System for present and future generations.

The
Globe
Pequot
Press

Guilford, Connecticut

Photo credits: title page, page 53 © Scott T. Smith; pages iii, 27, 29, 37, 61 © Tom Till; pages iv–v, 24–25 © Carr Clifton; pages 3, 6, 46–47, 49 © Fred Hirschmann; pages 9, 43, 52 © David Muench; pages 11, 15, 40 © Laurence Parent; pages 31, 34–35, 58 © Willard Clay; page 48 © Larry Ulrich

Maps: © Trails Illustrated, a division of National Geographic Maps
Cover and text design: Adam Schwartzman
Cover photo: Bass Harbor Head Light in Acadia National Park, Maine (© Laurence Parent)

Library of Congress Cataloging-in-Publication Data is available

ISBN 0-7627-0572-8

♲ Printed on recycled paper
Printed and bound in Quebec, Canada
First edition/First printing

National Parks
and Conservation Association

Thomas C. Kiernan
President

Dear Reader:

Welcome to the National Parks and Conservation Association's national park guidebooks—a series designed to help you to discover America's most significant scenery, history, and culture found in the more than 370 areas that make up the U.S. National Park System.

The park system represents the best America has to offer for our natural, historical, and cultural heritage—a collection of resources that we have promised to preserve "unimpaired" for future generations. We hope that, in addition to giving you practical information to help you plan your visits to national park areas, these guides also will help you be a more aware, more responsible visitor to our parks. The cautions offered at the beginning of these guides are not to frighten you away but to remind you that we all have a role in protecting the parks. For it is only if each and every one of us takes responsibility that these special places will be preserved and available for future generations to enjoy.

For more than three-quarters of a century, the National Parks and Conservation Association has been America's leading citizen advocacy group working solely to protect the national parks. Whether fighting to preserve the wilderness character of Cumberland Island National Seashore, preventing the expansion of a major airport outside the Everglades, stopping a coal mine at Cumberland Gap, or defeating legislation that could lead to the closure of many national parks, NPCA has made the voices of its members and supporters heard in efforts to protect the resources of our national parks from harm.

We hope that you will join in our commitment. Remember: when you visit the parks, take only pictures, and leave only footprints.

1776 Massachusetts Avenue, N.W., Washington, D.C. 20036-1904
Telephone (202) 223-NPCA(6722) • Fax (202) 659-0650
♻ PRINTED ON RECYCLED PAPER

CONTENTS

Northeast Region

ABBREVIATIONS

IHS	International Historic Site	NMP	National Military Park
NB	National Battlefield	NP	National Park
NBP	National Battlefield Park	NRA	National Recreation Area
NHP	National Historical Park	NS	National Seashore
NHS	National Historic Site	NSR	National Scenic River
N MEM	National Memorial	NST	National Scenic Trail
NM	National Monument	SRR	Scenic and Recreational River

0   100   200   Miles

0   100   200   300   Kilometers

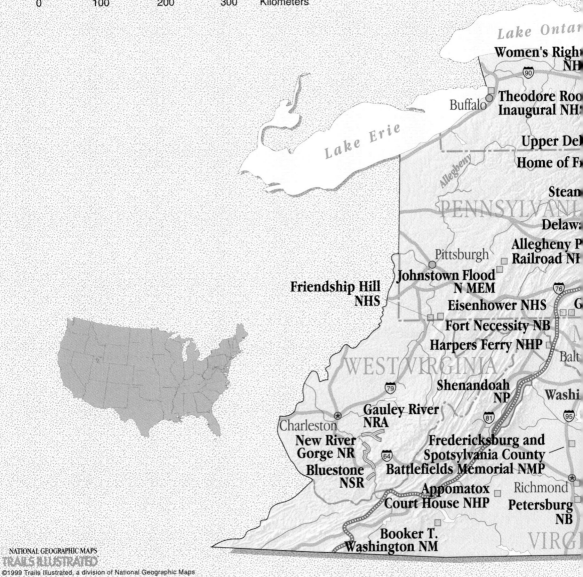

Lake Ontar

Women's Righ
NH

Theodore Roo
Inaugural NH

Buffalo

Lake Erie

Upper Del

Home of Fr

Allegheny

Stea

PENNSYLVANI

Delawa

Allegheny P
Railroad NI

Pittsburgh

Johnstown Flood
N MEM

Friendship Hill
NHS

Eisenhower NHS   G

Fort Necessity NB

Harpers Ferry NHP

WEST VIRGINIA

Balt

Shenandoah
NP   Washi

Gauley River
NRA

Charleston

New River
Gorge NR

Fredericksburg and
Spotsylvania County
Battlefields Memorial NMP

Bluestone
NSR

Appomatox
Court House NHP

Richmond

Petersburg
NB

Booker T.
Washington NM

VIRG

Maine Acadian
Culture Project

Appalachian
National Scenic
Trail

Saint Croix
Island
IHS

MAINE

Acadia NP

Augusta

Montpelier

NEW YORK   VT

Marsh- Billings-Rockefeller NHP

Saint Gaudens
NHS

Concord

Fort Stanwix
NM
Saratoga
NHP

Albany

NH

MA

Boston

Martin Van Buren
NHS

Roger Williams N MEM

Cape Cod NS

Springfield Armory NHS

Hartford

CT

Providence

Roosevelt NHS
or Roosevelt NHS

Vanderbilt Mansion
NHS

RI

re NSR

Weir Farm NHS

Gap NRA
orristown NHP

Edison NHS

New York

NJ

burg

NMP

Philadelphia

Great
Egg
Harbor
SRR

Dover

DE

rge
hington
hplace NM
d NBP

Assateague
Island NS

olonial NHP

BOSTON AREA

Adams NHP
Boston African American NHS
Boston NHP
F.L. Olmsted NHS
J.F. Kennedy NHS
Longfellow NHS
Lowell NHP
Minute Man NHP
Salem Maritime NHS
Saugus Iron Works NHS

NEW YORK CITY AREA

Castle Clinton NM
Federal Hall N MEM
Fire Island NS
Gateway NRA
General Grant N MEM
Hamilton Grange N MEM
Sagamore Hill NHS
Saint Paul's Chuch NHS
Statue of Liberty NM
The Lower East Side
    Tenement NHS
Theo Roosevelt Birthplace NHS

PHILADELPHIA AREA

E.A. Poe NHS
Hopewell Furnace NHS
Independence NHP
T. Kosciusko N MEM
Valley Forge NHP

BALTIMORE AREA

Fort McHenry NM and
    Historic Shrine
Hampton NHS

NATIONAL CAPITAL AREA

District of Columbia:

Constitution Gardens
Ford's Theatre NHS
Frederick Douglass NHS
Lincoln Memorial
L.B. Johnson Memorial
    Grove
Mary McLeod Bethune
    Council House NHS
National Capital Parks
National Mall
Pennsylvania Avenue NHS
Rock Creek Park
The White House
Theo. Roosevelt Island
Thos. Jefferson Memorial
Vietnam Veterans Memorial
Washington Monument

Maryland:

Antietam NB
Catoctin Mountain Park
C & O Canal NHP
Clara Barton NHS
Fort Washington Park
Greenbelt Park
Monocacy NB
Piscataway Park
Potomac Heritage NST
Thomas Stone NHS

Virginia:

Arlington House
George Washington
    Memorial Parkway
Maggie L. Walker NHS
Manassas NBP
Prince William Forest Park
Wolf Trap Farm Park

▲ Trees along Chesapeake and Ohio Canal National Historical Park, Maryland

GENERAL INFORMATION

Whether you're an American history buff or a birdwatcher, a lover of rocky coastlines or marshy swamps, a dedicated environmentalist or a weekend rambler, and whether you're seeking a way to spend a carefully planned month-long vacation or an unexpectedly free sunny afternoon—the national parks are for you. They offer a broad spectrum of natural and cultural resources in all 50 states as well as Guam, Puerto Rico, the Virgin Islands, and American Samoa where you can learn, exercise, participate in activities, and be constantly moved and inspired by the riches available. Perhaps most important of all, as one of the National Park System's 280 million annual visitors, you become part of the attempt to preserve our natural and historical treasures for present and future generations.

This guidebook will help you do that, as one in a series of eight Regional National Park Guides covering all the units in the National Park System. This section of general information provides both an overview of key facts that can be applied to every unit and a brief history of the National Parks and Conservation Association.

SPECIAL PARK PASSES

Some parks charge entrance fees to help offset their operational costs. Several options for special entrance passes are available, enabling you to choose the most appropriate and economical way for you and your family and friends to visit sites.

Park Pass: For this annual entrance permit to a specific fee-charging park, monument, historic site, or recreation area in the National Park System, the cost is usually $10 or $15 depending on the area. Such a pass does not cover any fees other than entrance for permit holder and any accompanying passengers in a private noncommercial vehicle or, in the case of walk-in facilities, the permit holder's spouse, children, and parents. The pass may be pur-

chased in person or by mail from the unit at which it will be used. It is nontransferable and nonrefundable.

Golden Eagle Passport: This annual entrance pass admits visitors to all the federal lands that charge entrance fees; these include national parks, monuments, historic sites, recreation areas, national forests, and national wildlife refuges. The pass costs $50 and is valid for one year from purchase. It does not cover any fees other than entrance for permit holder and any accompanying passengers in a private noncommercial vehicle or, in the case of walk-in facilities, the holder's spouse, children, and parents. The Golden Eagle Passport may be purchased in person or by mail from the National Park Service, Office of Public Inquiries, Room 1013, U.S. Department of the Interior, 18th & C Streets, N.W., Washington, DC 20240 (202-208-4747) or at any of the seven National Park Service field offices, any of the nine U.S. Forest Service regional offices, or any national park unit and other federal areas that charge an entrance fee. It is nontransferable and nonrefundable.

Golden Age Passport: A one-time $10 fee for this pass allows lifetime entrance to all federal fee-charging areas as described in the Golden Eagle Passport section for citizens and permanent residents of the United States who are 62 years of age or older and any accompanying passengers in a private noncommercial vehicle or, in the case of walk-in facilities, the holder's spouse and children. This pass also entitles the holder to a 50 percent discount on use fees charged in park areas. The Golden Age Passport must be obtained IN PERSON at any of the locations listed in the Golden Eagle Passport section; mail requests are not accepted. Applicants must provide proof of age, such as a driver's license or birth certificate, or sign an affidavit attesting to eligibility.

Golden Access Passport: This free lifetime entrance permit to all federal fee-charging areas as described in the Golden Eagle Passport section is available for citizens and permanent residents of the United States who are visually impaired or permanently disabled and any accompanying passengers in a private noncommercial vehicle or, in the case of walk-in facilities, the permit holder's spouse, children, and parents. It also entitles the holder to a 50 percent discount on use fees charged in park areas. The Golden Access Passport must be obtained IN PERSON at any of the locations listed in the Golden Eagle Passport section; mail requests are not accepted. Applicant must provide proof of eligibility to receive federal benefits or sign an affidavit attesting to one's eligibility.

PASSPORT TO YOUR NATIONAL PARKS

The *Passport to Your National Parks* is a special commemorative item designed to serve as a companion for park visitors. This informative and unique publication records each visit through special regional and national stamps and cancellations. When you visit any national park, be sure to have your Passport canceled with a rubber stamp marking the name of the park and the date you were there. The Passport gives you the opportunity to share and relive your journey through America's national parks and will become a travel record to cherish for years. Passports cost $4.95; a full set of ten national and regional stamps are $3.95. The national parks represented in the stamp set vary from year to year. For ordering information, call 800-821-2903, or write to Eastern National Park & Monument Association, 110 Hector Street, Suite 105, Conshohocken, PA 19428.

HELPFUL TRIP-PLANNING PUBLICATIONS

Two volumes offer descriptive text on the National Park System: *Exploring Our National Parks and Monuments,* by Devereux Butcher (ninth edition by Russell D. Butcher), and *Exploring Our National Historic Parks and Sites,* by Russell D. Butcher. These books feature descriptions and black-and-white photographs of more than 370 National Park System units. Both volumes also contain chapters on possible new parks, threats to the parks, a history of NPCA, and the national

park standards. To order, contact Roberts Rinehart Publishers, 6309 Monarch Park Place, Niwot, CO 80503; 800-352-1985 or 303-530-4400.

NPCA offers the following brochures at no charge: *The National Parks: How to Have a Quality Experience* and *Visiting Battlefields: The Civil War.* These brochures provide helpful information on how best to enjoy a visit to the national parks. NPCA members can also receive the *Park System Map and Guide, The National Parks Index, The National Parks Camping Guide,* and *Lesser Known Areas* as part of NPCA's PARK-PAK by calling 202-223-6722, ext. 214.

The Story Behind the Scenery® and *The Continuing Story®* series are lavishly illustrated books providing informative text and magnificent photographs of the landscapes, flora, and fauna of our national parklands. More than 100 titles on the national parks, historic events, and Indian cultures, as well as an annual national parks calendar, are available. For information, call toll free 800-626-9673, fax to 702-731-9421, or write to KC Publications, 3245 E. Patrick Lane, Suite A, Las Vegas, NV 89120.

The National Parks: Index and *Lesser Known Areas,* both produced by the National Park Service, can be ordered by contacting the Superintendent of Documents, U.S. Government Printing Office, Washington, DC 20402-9325; 202-512-1800. To receive at no charge the *National Park System Map and Guide,* the *National Trails System Map and Guide;* or an *Official Map and Guide* of specific national parks, contact National Park Service, Office of Information, P.O. Box 37127, Washington, DC 20013-7127; 202-208-4747.

National Parks Visitor Facilities and Services is a directory of vendors authorized to serve park visitors through contracts with the National Park Service. Concessionaires offering lodging, food, beverages, outfitting, tours, trail rides, and other activities and services are listed alphabetically. To order, contact the National Park Hospitality Association, 1331 Pennsylvania Ave., N.W., Suite 724, Washington, DC 20004; 202-662-7097.

▲ *The Thomas Jefferson Memorial at the Tidal Basin, District of Columbia*

Great Walks, Inc., publishes six pocket-sized books of detailed information on specific trails in Yosemite; Sequoia and Kings Canyon in California; Big Bend; Great Smoky Mountains; and Acadia and Mount Desert Island in Maine. For information, send $1 (refundable with your first order) to Great Walks, P.O. Box 410, Goffstown, NH 03045.

The U.S. Bureau of Land Management (BLM) offers free maps that detail recreation areas and scenic and backcountry roads and trails. These are available by contacting the BLM at the Department of the Interior, 1849 C St., N.W., Suite 5600, Washington, DC 20240; 202-452-5125. In addition, *Beyond the National Parks: A Recreational Guide to Public Lands in the West,* published by the Smithsonian Institution Press, is an informative guidebook to many spe-

cial places administered by BLM. *America's Secret Recreation Areas,* by Michael Hodgson, is an excellent resource for little-known natural areas in 12 Western states. It details 270 million acres of land administered by BLM, with campgrounds, recreational activities, trails, maps, facilities, and much more. The 1995-96 edition is published by Foghorn Press and is available for $17.95 by calling 1-800-FOGHORN.

The National Wildlife Refuge Visitors Guide can be ordered free from the U.S. Fish and Wildlife Service's Publications Unit at 4401 North Fairfax Dr., MS 130 Webb, Arlington, VA 22203; 703-358-1711.

The four-volume *Birds of the National Parks* by Roland H. Wauer, a retired NPS interpreter and biologist, provides an excellent reference on the parks' birds and their seasons and habitats. This series, written for the average rather than specialist park visitor, is unfortunately out of print.

SAFETY AND REGULATIONS

To protect the national parks' natural and cultural resources and the millions of people who come to enjoy them, the National Park Service asks every visitor to abide by some important regulations. Park staffs do all they can to help you have a safe and pleasant visit, but your cooperation is essential.

Some park hazards—deep lakes, sheer cliffs, extremely hot or cold temperatures—cannot be eliminated. However, accidents and illnesses can be prevented if you use the same common sense you would at home and become familiar with the park. Take some time before your trip or when you first arrive to get to know the park's regulations, warnings, and potential hazards. If you have children, make sure they understand such precautions, and keep a careful watch over them, especially in potentially dangerous situations. If you are injured or become ill, the staff can help by directing you to the nearest medical center and, in some parks, by giving you emergency care.

A few rules and safety tips are common to many parks. At all parks, you must keep your campsite clean and the park free of litter by disposing of refuse in trash receptacles. The National Park Service also asks you to follow federal regulations and refrain from the abuse of alcohol and the use of drugs, which are often contributing factors to injuries and deaths. Other rules and safety tips are outlined in the "Special Advisories and Visitor Ethics" section; more detailed information may be provided in park brochures, on signs, and on bulletin boards at camping areas and other park sites. The National Park Service asks that you report any violation of park regulations to park authorities. If you have any questions, seek the advice of a ranger.

SPECIAL ADVISORIES AND VISITOR ETHICS

Safe Driving

Park roads are designed for sightseeing, not speeding. Because roads are often narrow and winding and sometimes steep, visitors should drive carefully, observe posted speed limits, and be alert for wildlife, pedestrians, bicyclists, other drivers, fallen rocks or trees, slippery roads, and other hazards. Be especially alert for motorists who might stop unexpectedly for sightseeing or wildlife viewing. Visitors are urged to use roadside pullouts instead of stopping on the roadway.

Campfires

Most parks permit fires, as long as certain rules are followed. To avoid a wildfire that would be dangerous to people, property, and natural resources, parks may allow only certain types of campfires—fires only in grills provided, for example, or in designated fire rings. Firewood gathering may be prohibited or restricted to certain areas, so visitors should plan on bringing their own fuel supply. Fires should be kept under control, should never be left unattended, and should be thoroughly extinguished before departure.

Quiet Hours

Out of respect for other visitors, campers should keep noise to a minimum at all times, especially from 10 p.m. to 6 a.m.

Pets

Pets must always be leashed or otherwise physically restrained for the protection of the animal, other visitors, and wildlife. Pets may be prohibited from certain areas, including public buildings, trails, and the backcountry. A few parks prohibit pets altogether. Dog owners are responsible for keeping their pets quiet in camping areas and elsewhere. Guide dogs are exempted from park restrictions. Some parks provide kennel services; contact the park visitor center for information.

Protection of Valuables

Theft is just as much a problem in the national parks as elsewhere, so when leaving a campsite or heading out on a trail, visitors should take valuables along or hide them out-of-sight in a locked vehicle, preferably in the trunk.

Heat, Cold, and Other Hazards

Visitors should take precautions to deal with the demands and hazards of a park environment. On hot days, pace yourself, schedule strenuous activities for the morning and evening hours, and drink plenty of water and other fluids. On cold days or if you get cold and wet, frostbite and the life-threatening illness called hypothermia can occur, so avoid subjecting yourself to these conditions for long periods. In the thinner air of mountains and high plateaus, even those tasks easy to perform at home can leave one short of breath and dizzy; the best advice is to slow down. If a thunderstorm occurs, avoid exposed areas and open bodies of water, where lightning often strikes, and keep out of low-lying areas and stream beds, where flash floods are most likely to occur.

Wild Plants and Animals

It is the responsibility of every visitor to help preserve the native plants and animals protected in the parks: leave them as you find them, undisturbed and safe. Hunting or carrying a loaded weapon is prohibited in all national parks and national monuments. Hunting during the designated season is allowed in parts of only a few National Park System areas, such as national recreation areas, national preserves, and national seashores and lakeshores. While biting insects or toxic plants, such as poison ivy or poison oak, are the most likely danger you will encounter, visitors should be aware of hazards posed by other wild plants and animals. Rattlesnakes, ticks, and animals carrying rabies or other transmittable diseases, for instance, inhabit some parks. Any wild creature—whether it is as large as a bison or moose or as small as a raccoon or prairie dog—is unpredictable and should be viewed from a distance. Remember that feeding any wild animal is absolutely prohibited.

Campers should especially guard against attracting bears to their campsites as a close encounter with a grizzly, brown, or black bear can result in serious injury or death. Park officials in bear country recommend, and often require, that campers take certain precautions. One is to keep a campsite clean. Bears' sensitive noses can easily detect food left on cans, bottles, and utensils or even personal items with food-like odors (toothpaste, deodorant, etc.). Second, food items should be stored in containers provided by the parks or in your vehicle, preferably out of sight in the trunk. Bears, especially those in Yosemite, are adept at breaking into cars and other motor vehicles containing even small amounts of food and can cause extensive damage to motor vehicles as they attempt to reach what they can smell. Third, in the backcountry, food should be hung from poles or wires that are provided or from a tree; visitors should inquire at the park as to the recommended placement. In treeless surroundings, campers should store food at least 50 yards from any campsite. If bears inhabit a park on your itinerary, ask the National Park Service for a bear brochure with helpful tips on avoiding trouble in bear country and inquire if bears are a problem where you plan to hike or camp.

Backcountry Camping

Camping in the remote backcountry of a park requires much more preparation than other camping. Most parks require that you pick up a backcountry permit before your trip so that rangers will know about your plans. They can also advise you of hazards and regulations and give you up-to-date information on road, trail, river, lake, or sea conditions, weather forecasts, special fire regulations, availability of water, and other matters. Backcountry permits are available at visitor centers, headquarters, and ranger stations.

There are some basic rules to follow whenever you camp in the backcountry: stay on the trails; pack out all trash; obey fire regulations; be prepared for sudden and drastic weather changes; carry a topographic map or nautical chart when necessary; and carry plenty of food and water. In parks where water is either unavailable or scarce, you may need to carry as much as one gallon of water per person per day. In other parks, springs, streams, or lakes may be abundant, but always purify water before drinking it. Untreated water can carry contaminants. One of the most common, especially in Western parks, is *giardia*, an organism that causes an unpleasant intestinal illness. Water may have to be boiled or purified with tablets; check with the park staff for the most effective treatment.

Sanitation

Visitors should bury human waste six to eight inches below ground and a minimum of 100 feet from a watercourse. Waste water should be disposed of at least 100 feet from a watercourse or campsite. Do not wash yourself, your clothing, or your dishes in any watercourse.

CAMPING RESERVATIONS

Most campsites are available on a first-come, first-served basis, but many sites can be reserved through the National Park Reservation Service. For reservations at Acadia, Assateague Island, Cape Hatteras, Channel Islands, Chickasaw, Death Valley, Everglades, Glacier, Grand Canyon, Great Smoky Mountains, Greenbelt, Gulf Islands, Joshua Tree, Katmai, Mount Rainier, Rocky Mountain, Sequoia-Kings Canyon, Sleeping Bear Dunes, Shenandoah, Whiskeytown, and

▲ *The U.S.S.* **Constitution,** *Boston, Massachusetts*

Zion, call 800-365-CAMP. For reservations for Yosemite National Park, call 800-436-PARK. Reservations can also be made at any of these parks in person. Currently, reservations can be made as much as eight weeks in advance or up to the day before the start of a camping stay. Please have credit card and detailed camping information available when you call in order to facilitate the reservation process.

BIOSPHERE RESERVES AND WORLD HERITAGE SITES

A number of the national park units have received international recognition by the United Nations Educational, Scientific and Cultural Organization for their superlative natural and/or cultural values. Biosphere Reserves are representative examples of diverse natural landscapes, with both a fully protected natural core or park unit and surrounding land being managed to meet human needs. World Heritage Sites include natural and cultural sites with "universal" values that illustrate significant geological processes, may be crucial to the survival of threatened plants and animals, or demonstrate outstanding human achievement.

CHECKLIST FOR HIKING AND CAMPING

Clothing

Rain gear (jacket and pants)
Windbreaker
Parka
Thermal underwear
T-shirt
Long pants and shorts
Extra wool shirt and/or sweater
Hat with brim
Hiking boots
Camp shoes/sneakers
Wool mittens
Lightweight shoes

Equipment

First-aid kit
Pocket knife
Sunglasses
Sunscreen
Topographic map
Compass
Flashlight, fresh batteries, spare bulb
Extra food & water (even for short hikes)
Waterproof matches
Fire starter
Candles
Toilet paper
Digging tool for toilet needs
Day backpack
Sleeping bag
Sleeping pad or air mattress
Tarp/ground sheet
Sturdy tent, preferably free-standing
Insect repellent
Lip balm
Pump-type water filter/water purification tablets
Water containers
Plastic trash bags
Biodegradable soap
Small towel
Toothbrush
Lightweight backpack stove/extra fuel
Cooking pot(s)
Eating utensils
Can opener
Electrolyte replacement for plain water (e.g., Gatorade)
Camera, film, lenses, filters
Binoculars
Sewing kit
Lantern
Nylon cord (50 feet)
Whistle
Signal mirror

▲ Forge on the Saugus Iron Works National Historic Site, Massachusetts

A Brief History of the National Parks and Conservation Association

In 1916, when Congress established the National Park Service to administer the then nearly 40 national parks and monuments, the agency's first director, Stephen Tyng Mather, quickly saw the need for a private organization, independent of the federal government, to be the citizens' advocate for the parks.

Consequently, on May 19, 1919, the National Parks Association—later renamed the National Parks and Conservation Association (NPCA)—was founded in Washington, D.C. The National Park Service's former public relations director, Robert Sterling Yard, was named to lead the new organization—a position he held for a quarter century.

The association's chief objectives were then and continue to be the following: to vigorously oppose threats to the integrity of the parks; to advocate worthy and consistent standards of *national* significance for the addition of new units to the National Park System; and, through a variety of educational means, to promote the public understanding and appreciation of the parks. From the beginning, threats to the parks have been a major focus of the organization. One of the biggest conservation battles of NPCA's earliest years erupted in 1920, when Montana irrigation interests advocated building a dam and raising the level of Yellowstone Lake in Yellowstone National Park. Fortunately, this threat to the world's first national park was ultimately defeated—the first landmark victory of the fledgling citizens' advocacy group on behalf of the national parks.

At about the same time, a controversy developed over the authority given to the Water Power Commission (later renamed the Federal Power Commission) to authorize the construction of hydropower projects in national parks. The commission had already approved the flooding of Hetch Hetchy Valley in Yosemite National Park. In the ensuing political struggle, NPCA pushed for an amendment to the water power law that would prohibit such projects in

all national parks. A compromise produced only a partial victory: the ban applied to the parks then in existence, but not to parks yet to be established. As a result, each new park's enabling legislation would have to expressly stipulate that the park was exempt from the commission's authority to develop hydropower projects. Yet this success, even if partial, was significant.

Also in the 1920s, NPCA successfully urged establishment of new national parks: Shenandoah, Great Smoky Mountains, Carlsbad Caverns, Bryce Canyon, and a park that later became Kings Canyon, as well as an expanded Sequoia. The association also pushed to expand Yellowstone, Grand Canyon, and Rocky Mountain national parks, pointing out that "the boundaries of the older parks were often established arbitrarily, following ruler lines drawn in far-away offices." The association continues to advocate such topographically and ecologically oriented boundary improvements for many parks.

In 1930, the establishment of Colonial National Historical Park and the George Washington Birthplace National Monument signaled a broadening of the National Park System to places of primarily historical rather than environmental importance. A number of other historical areas, such as Civil War battlefields, were soon transferred from U.S. military jurisdiction to the National Park Service, and NPCA accurately predicted that this new category of parks "will rapidly surpass, in the number of units, its world-celebrated scenic" parks. Today, there are roughly 200 historical parks out of the total of 378 units. NPCA also pushed to add other units, including Everglades National Park, which was finally established in 1947.

A new category of National Park System units was initiated with the establishment of Cape Hatteras National Seashore in North Carolina. However, in spite of NPCA opposition, Congress permitted public hunting in the seashore—a precedent that subsequently opened the way to allow this consumptive resource use in other national seashores, national lakeshores, national rivers, and national preserves. With the exception of traditional, subsistence hunting in Alaska national preserves, NPCA continues to oppose hunting in all national parks and monuments.

In contrast to its loss at Cape Hatteras, NPCA achieved a victory regarding Kings Canyon National Park as a result of patience and tenacity. When the park was established in 1940, two valleys—Tehipite and Cedar Grove—were left out of the park as a concession to hydroelectric power and irrigation interests. A few years later, however, as the result of concerted efforts by the association and other environmental groups, these magnificently scenic valleys were added to the park.

In 1942, the association took a major step in its public education mission when it began publishing National Parks. This award-winning, full-color magazine contains news, editorials, and feature articles that help to inform members about the parks, threats facing them, and opportunities for worthy new parks and offers readers a chance to participate in the protection and enhancement of the National Park System.

In one of the most heavily publicized park-protection battles of the 1950s, NPCA and other groups succeeded in blocking construction of two hydroelectric power dams that would have inundated the spectacularly scenic river canyons in Dinosaur National Monument. In the 1960s, an even bigger battle erupted over U.S. Bureau of Reclamation plans to build two dams in the Grand Canyon. But with the cooperative efforts of a number of leading environmental organizations and tremendous help from the news media, these schemes were defeated, and Grand Canyon National Park was expanded.

In 1980, the National Park System nearly tripled in size with the passage of the Alaska National Interest Lands Conservation Act (ANILCA). One of the great milestones in the history of American land conservation, ANILCA established ten new, and expanded three existing, national park units in Alaska. This carefully crafted compromise also recognized the special circumstances of Alaska and authorized subsistence hunting, fishing, and gathering by rural residents as well as special access provisions on most units. The challenge of ANILCA is to achieve a balance of interests that are often in conflict. Currently, NPCA is working to protect sensitive park areas and wildlife from inappropriate development of roads and unregulated motorized use, and to ensure that our magnificent national parks in

Alaska always offer the sense of wildness, discovery, and adventure that Congress intended.

In 1981, the association sponsored a conference to address serious issues affecting the welfare of the National Park System. The following year, NPCA published a book on this theme called National Parks in Crisis. In the 1980s and 1990s, as well, the association sponsored its nationwide "March for Parks" program in conjunction with Earth Day in April. Money raised from the hundreds of marches funds local park projects, including improvement and protection priorities and educational projects in national, state, and local parks.

NPCA's landmark nine-volume document, National Park System Plan, was issued in 1988. It contained proposals for new parks and park expansions, assessments of threats to park resources and of research needs, explorations of the importance of interpretation to the visitor's quality of experience, and issues relating to the internal organization of the National Park Service. Two years later, the two-volume Visitor Impact Management was released. This document found favor within the National Park Service because of its pragmatic discussions of "carrying capacity" and visitor-impact management methodology and its case studies. In 1993, Park Waters in Peril was released, focusing on threats seriously jeopardizing water resources and presenting a dozen case studies.

The association has become increasingly concerned about the effect of noise on the natural quiet in the parks. NPCA has helped formulate restrictions on flightseeing tours over key parts of the Grand Canyon; urged special restrictions on tour flights over Alaska's national parks; supported a ban on tour flights over other national parks such as Yosemite; expressed opposition to plans for construction of major new commercial airports close to Mojave National Preserve and Petroglyph National Monument; opposed the recreational use of snowmobiles in some parks and advocated restrictions on their use in others; and supported regulations prohibiting the use of personal watercraft on lakes in national parks.

Other association activities of the late 20th century have included helping to block development of a major gold mining operation that could have seriously impaired Yellowstone National Park; opposing a coal mine near

Zion National Park that would have polluted Zion Canyon's North Fork of the Virgin River; objecting to proposed lead mining that could pollute the Ozark National Scenic Riverways; opposing a major waste dump adjacent to Joshua Tree National Park; and helping to defeat a proposed U.S. Department of Energy nuclear waste dump adjacent to Canyonlands National Park and on lands worthy of addition to the park. NPCA is currently proposing the completion of this national park with the addition of 500,000 acres. This proposal to double the size of the park would extend protection across the entire Canyonlands Basin. NPCA has also continued to work with the Everglades Coalition and others to help formulate meaningful ways of restoring the seriously impaired Everglades ecosystem; is urging protection of New Mexico's geologically and scenically outstanding Valles Caldera, adjacent to Bandelier National Monument; and is pushing for the installation of scrubbers on air-polluting coal-fired power plants in the Midwest and upwind from the Grand Canyon.

The association, in addition, is continuing to seek meaningful solutions to traffic congestion and urbanization on the South Rim of the Grand Canyon and in Yosemite Valley; is opposing construction of a six-lane highway through Petroglyph National Monument that would destroy sacred Native American cultural assets; and is fighting a plan to build a new road through Denali National Park. NPCA has supported re-establishment of such native wildlife as the gray wolf at Yellowstone and desert bighorn sheep at Capitol Reef and other desert parks, as well as urging increased scientific research that will enable the National Park Service to more effectively protect natural ecological processes in the future. The association is also continuing to explore a proposal to combine Organ Pipe Cactus National Monument and Cabreza Prieta National Wildlife Refuge into a Sonoran Desert National Park, possibly in conjunction with Mexico's Pinacate Biosphere Reserve.

In 1994, on the occasion of NPCA's 75th anniversary, the association sponsored a major conference on the theme "Citizens Protecting America's Parks: Joining Forces for the Future." As a result, NPCA became more active in recruiting a more racially and socially diverse group of park protectors. Rallying new constituencies for the parks helped NPCA in 1995 to defeat a bill that would have called for Congress to review national parks for possible closure. NPCA was also instrumental in the passage of legislation to establish the National Underground Railroad Network to Freedom.

In January 1999, NPCA hosted another major conference, this time focusing on the need for the park system, and the Park Service itself, to be relevant, accessible, and open to all Americans. The conference led to the creation of a number of partnership teams between national parks and minority communities. In conjunction with all this program activity, the association experienced its greatest growth in membership, jumping from about 24,000 in 1980 to nearly 400,000 in the late 1990s.

As NPCA and its committed Board of Trustees, staff, and volunteers face the challenges of park protection in the 21st century, the words of the association's past president, Wallace W. Atwood, in 1929 are as timely now as then:

All who join our association have the satisfaction that comes only from unselfish acts; they will help carry forward a consistent and progressive program . . . for the preservation and most appropriate utilization of the unique wonderlands of our country. Join and make this work more effective.

Each of us can help nurture one of the noblest endeavors in the entire history of mankind—the national parks idea that began so many years ago at Yellowstone and has spread and blossomed around the world. Everyone can help make a difference in determining just how well we succeed in protecting the priceless and irreplaceable natural and cultural heritage of the National Park System and passing it along unimpaired for the generations to come.

ACADIA NATIONAL PARK

▲ *Bass Harbor Head Light*

ACADIA NATIONAL PARK

P.O. Box 177
Bar Harbor, ME 04609-0177
207-288-3338 or 288-9561

This 46,998-acre national park on the rugged Atlantic coast of "Down East" Maine protects an exquisitely beautiful and ecologically varied area. The park is mostly located on Mount Desert Island, named "L'Isle des Monts-desert" (the island of barren mountains) in 1604 by French explorer Samuel de Champlain and the largest island along the coast of Maine. In addition, the park includes a mainland unit on Schoodic Peninsula and a number of smaller offshore islands, such as Baker, Bald Porcupine, Sheep Porcupine, and Little Moose, as well as parts of Isle au Haut and Little Cranberry, Bear, and Bar islands.

The park's landscape is varied. In a spectacular range of parallel, glacially rounded, sheer-cliffed mountain ridges, seven largely barren granite summits rise more than a thousand feet and provide magnificent views of the island-dotted sea. Between these mountains, numerous mountain- and forest-framed lakes and ponds occupy glacier-carved basins and valleys. Brooks and waterfalls splash down the mountainsides, and a long arm of the sea—the only fjord on the U.S. Atlantic coast—extends between the mountains, nearly cutting Mount Desert Island in half. Forests, containing a rich blend of coniferous and deciduous trees, offer diverse habitats for an abundance of wildlife. Elsewhere are arctic-like peat-bogs, freshwater- and salt-marshes, a sandy ocean beach, and rocky ocean ledges and cliffs where storms create surf that crashes in thundering "geysers" of spray.

More than 120 miles of trails offer rewarding opportunities for hiking, while 44 miles of gravel carriage roads winding through the park's eastern part offer delightful routes for hiking and bicycling in summer and cross-country skiing and snowshoeing in winter. Canoeing on the lakes and ponds, sailing on the bays, and taking boat trips to outer islands are other ways to enjoy the wonder of this paradise. In late spring and early summer, the woodlands of Acadia are magically flooded with a chorus of bird songs. In late September and the first week of October, the woods are set ablaze with the vibrant shades of red, orange, and yellow of autumn foliage.

The park's predecessor, Sieur de Monts National Monument, was established in 1916; in 1919, it was redesignated Lafayette National Park; and in 1929, the name was changed to Acadia National Park. Virtually all of the land within the park has been generously donated by private individuals, including John D. Rockefeller, Jr., who gave more than 11,000 acres that include the beautifully designed network of carriage paths he had previously built. In 1993, with the help of a corporate partner, NPCA contributed nearly $10,000 to help restore these gravel roads. The organization also supported establishment of an officially designated, permanent boundary for Acadia—a goal that was finally achieved in 1986.

OUTSTANDING FEATURES

Among the outstanding features along the 20-mile Park Loop Road, on the *east side of Mount Desert Island* are: **Sieur de Monts Spring**, a beautiful sylvan spot highlighted by the Abbe Museum, presenting exhibits of Indian artifacts; the **Nature Center**, which presents natural history exhibits; **Acadia Wild Garden**, a display of native wildflowers, ferns, and other plantlife; **Schooner Head Overlook**, a rocky headland that can be viewed from the end of a short spur road, along with a view of island-dotted Frenchman Bay beyond; **Sand Beach** in Newport Cove, the park's only sandy beach, hemmed in by Great Head; **The Beehive**, a 520-foot summit reached by a steep trail that leads to a small pond called The Bowl; **Thunder Hole**, a deep cleft in the shore cliffs, where ocean surf often slams in with such force as to cause a deep, muffled booming sound; **Otter Cliffs**, the highest ocean cliffs on the U.S. Atlantic coast; **Otter Point**, a pine- and spruce-forested point jutting into the Atlantic, with views of outer islands to the south and of Otter Cove and Cadillac and Dorr mountains to the northwest; **Jordan Pond**, a sparkling, mile-long lake cradled in a valley beneath the cliffs of Penobscot and Pemetic mountains; **Jordan Pond House**, a seasonal, park concession-operated restaurant, serving lunch, afternoon tea-and-popovers, and dinner, thus continuing the tradition of the charming, rambling, rustic structure on this spot that operated from 1847 until it burned down in 1979; **The Bubbles**, the rocky, twin summits that rise from the north end of Jordan Pond; **Bubble Pond**, a jewel of a little lake framed by the steep, forested slopes of Cadillac and Pemetic mountains; and **Cadillac Mountain**, whose mostly barren, glacier-smoothed, granite summit, at 1,530-feet above sea level, is the highest point on the Atlantic Coast of the Americas north of Brazil.

Elsewhere on the east side of Mount Desert Island are the following: **Eagle Lake**, the largest body of water on this side of the island and providing a beautiful view of the mountains from the lake's northern end just off State Route 233; **Upper Hadlock Pond**, an exquisitely beautiful, mountain-framed pond located a mile north of Northeast Harbor on State Route 198; and **Somes Sound**, a four-mile-long arm of the sea that forms the only fjord on the United States East Coast, offering views that are especially beautiful from Sargeant Drive (which allows no trucks or trailers) along the sound's eastern shore.

On the west side of Mount Desert Island are the following: **Echo Lake**, a 1.5-mile-long lake, at the southern end of which is a beach, reached on a spur road from State Route 102, where swimming is popular (swimming in most of the island's other lakes and ponds is prohibited, as they are municipal water supplies); **Seawall**, a place often ideal for watching seabirds where smoothly rounded cobblestones have been pushed up by the ocean surf; **Ship Harbor**, an intimate, sheltered cove where the ocean's tides flow in and out; and **Bass Harbor Head Lighthouse**, which is atop the cliffs at the southernmost tip of Mount Desert Island and one of the East Coast's most photographed lighthouses.

Scenic features in *other units of the park* include the following: **Schoodic Peninsula**, a magical, 2,000-acre area of surf-pounded, pink-granite ledges and cliffs, sheltered coves, cobblestone beaches and seawalls, miniature

mountain summits, and fragrant forests of pine and spruce—the intimacy and delicacy of which contrasts with the awesome vastness of the open sea; located on the mainland across Frenchman Bay, to the east of Mount Desert Island; **Islesford Historical Museum**, which is a ferry ride away from Mount Desert Island's Northeast Harbor on Little Cranberry Island, presenting exhibits of ship models, tools, and photographs that reveal island life in the 19th and early 20th centuries; and **Isle au Haut**, a wild, outer coastal island that rises boldly out of the sea, as its French name implies, to 543 feet atop Mount Champlain, about 15 miles to the southwest of Mount Desert Island and reached by ferry from Stonington at the south end of State Route 15; a 3,000-acre part of the park protects roughly two-thirds of this island.

PRACTICAL INFORMATION

When to Go

The park is open year-round. In summer, high temperatures are often 70 to 80 degrees, but cooler days result from rain and coastal fog. In mid- to late-spring and early to mid-autumn, highs usually range from the 40s to 60s. Spectacular autumn foliage is one of the visual highlights of the year, usually climaxing during the first ten days or so of October. In winter, which lasts from November to April, highs are generally in the 30s; nighttime lows frequently plunge below zero. Annual snowfall is about 60 inches, but storms along the coast often start as snow and turn to rain or begin as rain and end with snow.

How to Get There

By Car: From Bangor, take U.S. Route 1A south to Ellsworth and then State Route 3 south onto Mount Desert Island. From Portland, take I-95 to Brunswick, U.S. Route 1 northeast to Ellsworth, and State Route 3 south onto Mount Desert.

By Air: Bar Harbor/Hancock County Airport (207-667-7329) is served by Colgan Air. Bangor International Airport (207-947-0384) and Portland International Jetport (207-774-7301) are served by most major carriers.

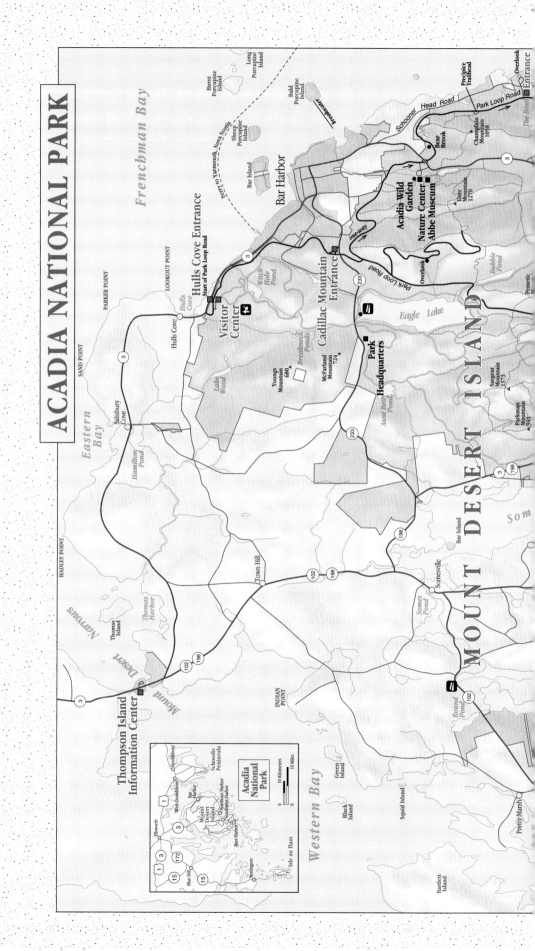

ACADIA NATIONAL PARK

Frenchman Bay

Eastern Bay

Long Porcupine Island

Burnt Porcupine Island

Sheep Porcupine Island

Bald Porcupine Island

Ferry to Yarmouth, Nova Scotia

Bar Island

Bar Harbor

Breakneck

SAND POINT

PARKER POINT

LOOKOUT POINT

Hulls Cove

Hulls Cove

Hulls Cove Entrance
Start of Park Loop Road

Visitor Center

Witch Hole Pond

Breakneck Ponds

Lake Wood

Youngs Mountain 680

Cadillac Mountain Entrance

McFarland Mountain 724

Aunt Betty Pond

Park Headquarters

one-way

Park Loop Road

Overlook

Acadia Wild Garden

Nature Center

Abbe Museum

Dorr Mountain 1270

Schooner Head Road

Park Loop Road

Breakwater

Bear Brook

Precipice Trailhead

Overlook

Entrance

Champlain Mountain 1058

The Beehive

3

3

Eagle Lake

Bubble Pond

Penetic

Sargent Mountain 1373

Parkman Mountain 941

Som

M O U N T   D E S E R T   I S L A N D

233

233

198

3

198

198

102

198

Bar Island

Somesville

Somes Pond

102

Salisbury Cove

Hamilton Pond

3

Town Hill

102

INDIAN POINT

Round Pond

Thomas Harbor

Thomas Island

HADLEY POINT

Narrows

Mount Desert

3

Thompson Island Information Center

198

102

Western Bay

Green Island

Black Island

Squid Island

Pretty Marsh

Bartlett Island

Acadia National Park

10 Kilometers

10 Miles

Ellsworth

1

3

172

15

Blue Hill

15

Gouldsboro

Schoodic Peninsula

West Gouldsboro

Bar Harbor

Mount Desert Island

Northeast Harbor

Southwest Harbor

Bass Harbor

Stonington

Isle au Haut

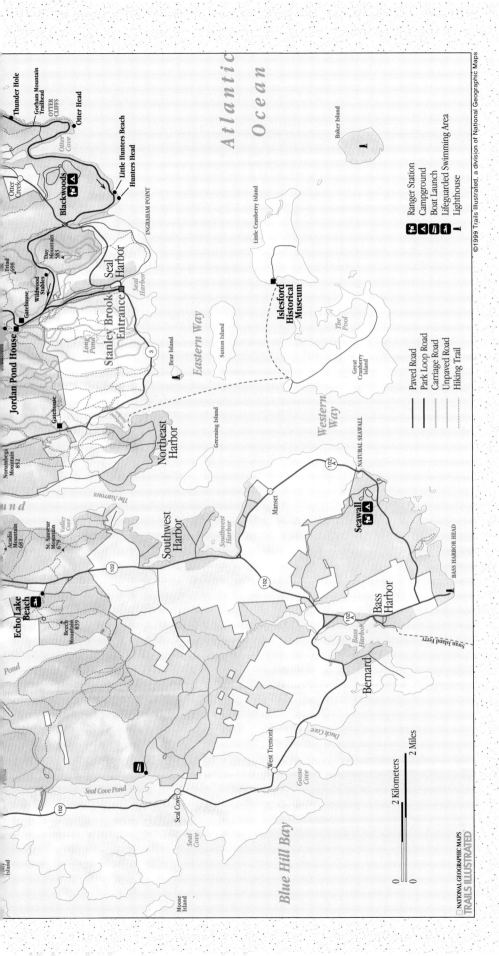

Atlantic Ocean

Thunder Hole
Gorham Mountain Trailhead
OTTER CLIFFS
Otter Head
Otter Cove

Otter Creek

Little Hunters Beach
Hunters Head

Blackwoods

INGRAHAM POINT

Day Mountain 583
Triad 698

Wildwood Stables

Seal Harbor

Gatehouse

Stanley Brook Entrance

Seal Harbor

Jordan Pond House

Gatehouse

Long Pond

3

Eastern Way

Bear Island

Sutton Island

Baker Island

Little Cranberry Island

Islesford Historical Museum

The Pool

Great Cranberry Island

Norumbega Mountain 852

Northeast Harbor

Greening Island

The Narrows

Western Way

Acadia Mountain 681
St. Sauveur Mountain 679
Valley Cove

Southwest Harbor

Southwest Harbor

Manset

NATURAL SEAWALL

102 A

Seawall

BASS HARBOR HEAD

Echo Lake Beach

Beech Mountain 839

Pond

102

102

102 A

Bass Harbor

Bass Harbor

Swan Island Ferry

Bernard

Seal Cove Pond

West Tremont

Duck Cove

Goose Cove

Seal Cove

Seal Cove

Blue Hill Bay

Moose Island

102

Pond

Island

Legend:
Paved Road
Park Loop Road
Carriage Road
Unpaved Road
Hiking Trail

Ranger Station
Campground
Boat Launch
Lifeguarded Swimming Area
Lighthouse

2 Kilometers
2 Miles
0
0

NATIONAL GEOGRAPHIC MAPS
TRAILS ILLUSTRATED

©1999 Trails Illustrated, a division of National Geographic Maps

19

By Train: There is no passenger rail service to or near the park.

By Bus: An island-wide transportation system on Mount Desert Island is being established. New England Transit Company (207-772-6587) travels between Boston and Bar Harbor from mid-June to Labor Day. Downeast Transportation (207-667-5796) travels year-round between Bar Harbor and Ellsworth.

By Boat: For passenger ferry service from Northeast Harbor to the Islesford Historical Museum on Little Cranberry Island, call Beal & Bunker, Inc., at 207-244-3575; and for the ferry from Southwest Harbor, call Cranberry Cove Boating Company at 207-244-5882. For passenger ferry service from Stonington to Isle au Haut, call Isle au Haut Ferry Company at 207-367-5193. For car ferry service to and from Yarmouth, Nova Scotia, Canada, from May through October, call Bay Ferries, Ltd. at 207-288-3395.

Fees and Permits

Entrance fees for the Park Loop Road are $10 per motor vehicle for a seven-day pass from May to November or $20 for a 12-month pass. Both are issued at the entrance station to this tour road or at the visitor center.

Visitor Center, Information Center, Museum, and Nature Center

Hulls Cove Visitor Center: open from May 1 to October 31. Information, interpretive exhibits, an orientation film, publications, schedules of naturalist activities, self-guided tape tours, and maps.

Thompson Island Information Center: open in summer. Information, publications, and maps.

Islesford Historical Museum: open daily, mid-June to Labor Day. Exhibits of 19th- and early 20th-century ship models, tools, and historic photographs.

Abbe Museum: open daily, May 1 to October 31. Indian artifacts and other exhibits.

Nature Center: open daily, mid-June through September. Natural history exhibits and publications.

Facilities

General stores are within one mile of Blackwoods and Seawall campgrounds. Supplies are also available in Bar Harbor, Northeast Harbor, Southwest Harbor, and Ellsworth. Service stations are located in Bar Harbor, Northeast Harbor, Southwest Harbor, and elsewhere on Mount Desert Island; repair services are available in Bar Harbor and Ellsworth.

The visitor center at Hulls Cove provides a mailbox. A full-service post office is located at 55 Cottage St., Bar Harbor. Other post offices are in Seal Harbor, Northeast Harbor, Somesville, and Southwest Harbor. Federal Express, at 43 Cottage St., serves Bar Harbor. Banks are located in Bar Harbor, Northeast Harbor, and Southwest Harbor.

Handicapped Accessibility

Park headquarters, Thompson and Fabbri Islands picnic sites, the nature center, several campsites and restrooms at Blackwoods and Seawall campgrounds, gift shops and restrooms on Cadillac Mountain and at the Jordan Pond House, restrooms at the Wendell Gilley Museum, and some trails and boat cruises are wheelchair-accessible. Two of the carriages used on carriage rides have lock-downs for wheelchairs. Access to parking and restrooms at the visitor center and Echo Lake Beach may require assistance. Contact the park for detailed information about accessibility.

Medical Services

First aid is available in the park. Mount Desert Island Hospital is located on the east side of the island in Bar Harbor, and other medical facilities are on the west side of the island in Southwest Harbor.

Pets

Pets must be attended and under physical restraint at all times; maximum leash length is six feet. Pets are not allowed on beaches or mountain ladder trails, inside public buildings, or at naturalist programs. There is no kennel service at the park. Veterinary care is available in Bar Harbor.

Safety and Regulations

For your safety and enjoyment and for the protection of the park, please follow these regulations and suggestions:

- Visitors are cautioned that shore ledges and cliff edges are slippery when wet and that crashing surf can catch unsuspecting persons by surprise.

- On mountain trails, watch your footing and know the limits of your stamina.

- Hikers are asked to refrain from smoking on trails and carriage roads to help prevent forest fires and to pack out all litter.

- Fires and camping are permitted only in designated sites.

- Remember that feeding, disturbing, capturing, or hunting wildlife, as well as collecting marine life and damaging or removing other natural and historic features, are prohibited in the park.

- Some of Mount Desert Island's lakes and ponds, such as Eagle Lake and Jordan, Bubble, and Upper and Lower Hadlock ponds, are municipal water supplies, in which swimming is prohibited.

ACTIVITIES

Options include hiking, birdwatching, interpreter-led walks and talks, bicycling, horseback riding, horse-drawn carriage rides, canoeing, kayaking, boating, sailing, boat tours, swimming, freshwater and saltwater fishing, cross-country skiing, snow-shoeing, ice-skating, snowmobiling, and ice-fishing. Further information is available in the park's newspaper, *Beaver Log*.

Hiking Trails

Among Acadia's many hiking trails, ranging from easy lowland paths to steep mountain routes, are the following:

On the east side of Mount Desert Island:
Great Head Trail, a mostly fairly easy, .8-mile walk to the 145-foot summit of Great

Head or a 1.4-mile loop beginning at Sand Beach parking area just off the Park Loop Road and affording views of island-dotted Frenchman Bay and the open ocean; **The Beehive Trail**, a 1.2-mile loop that is very precipitous and steep with iron ladders mounted in the rock by the ledges route (not recommended for persons fearing sheer drop-offs) or a moderate climb with several steep sections on the easier route, both beginning on the opposite side of the Park Loop Road from Sand Beach parking area and providing views of Sand Beach, Newport Cove, Great Head, and Frenchman Bay and the open ocean beyond; another trail branches from the Beehive, leads a short distance to a small pond, The Bowl, and continues on up the long southern ridge of 1,058-foot-high Champlain Mountain; **Ocean Drive Shore Path**, an easy 1.8-mile route between Sand Beach parking area and the southern tip of Otter Point, beginning at either end or at one of a number of parking areas along the Park Loop Road and affording excellent views of surf-pounded ocean ledges and Otter Cliffs; **Gorham Mountain Trail**, an easy to moderately steep, one-mile route to this 525-foot summit, beginning at Gorham Mountain parking area just beyond Thunder Hole on the Park Loop Road and providing views of Frenchman Bay, Otter Point, and Baker and the Cranberry islands beyond; **Cadillac Mountain South Ridge Trail**, a mostly easy-to-moderate, 3.5-mile route between the open, granite expanses of 1,530-foot-high Cadillac Mountain's summit and Blackwoods Campground and providing magnificent panoramas of mountains and the ocean; branching from this trail is the strenuous, .9-mile trail descending steeply down the west face of Cadillac Mountain to the northern end of Bubble Pond; **Bubble Pond-Pemetic Mountain Trail**, a mostly moderately steep, 1.2-mile route beginning at the northern end of Bubble Pond, climbing through a cathedral-like red-spruce forest, and reaching the open, glacially rounded, granite summit of this 1,248-foot mountain, from which are magnificent views of Eagle Lake, Jordan Pond, other mountains, and the island-dotted ocean; **South Bubble Trail**, a moderately steep, .7-mile route beginning at the second of two

Bubbles parking areas (at 1.6 miles north of the Jordan Pond House on the Park Loop Road), climbing through an old-growth beech, maple, and birch forest to the exposed, rocky, 766-foot summit of the South Bubble, on which is perched a huge boulder, and then providing a spectacular view southward down the length of Jordan Pond framed by Pemetic Mountain to the east and Penobscot Mountain's Jordan Cliffs to the west; **Jordan Pond Loop Trail**, a mostly easy, 3.3-mile route beginning and ending at the Penobscot Mountain parking area just northeast of the Jordan Pond House or at the first of two Bubbles parking areas, 1.4 miles north of Jordan Pond House on the Park Loop Road, and closely following the shore of this mountain-framed pond; **Jordan Pond House to Penobscot and Sargent Mountains Trail**, a moderate to fairly steep, 1.5-mile climb beginning at the Penobscot parking area just northeast of the Jordan Pond House, switchbacking up the cliffs of Jordan Ridge, suddenly emerging onto the exposed ridgetop expanse, and following the ridge to the 1,194-foot Penobscot summit, from which are unobstructed views eastward of Jordan Pond below and the Bubbles and Pemetic and Cadillac mountains beyond, and southward to the island-dotted ocean; from there, the trail drops into a mountain saddle coming in a quarter-mile to exquisite Sargent Mountain Pond, and climbing on for .75-mile to the open, rocky, 1,373-foot summit of Sargent Mountain, the island's second highest point.

On the west side of Mount Desert Island: **Acadia Mountain Trail**, a fairly strenuous, one-mile route beginning at the Acadia Mountain parking area just off State Route 102 (about three miles south of Somesville or three miles north of Southwest Harbor), climbing abruptly up steep granite ledges while winding through groves of picturesque red and pitch pines and small clumps of rare bear oak, and reaching the 681-foot summit of Acadia Mountain, from which is a magnificent, pine-framed panorama eastward of the entire length of Somes Sound with Norumbega (Brown) Mountain beyond; hikers wishing to avoid returning by the same route can follow a trail that descends very steeply off the south end of Acadia Mountain and connects, in .6-of-a-mile, with the old Man o' War Road; this latter road-

way leads back to the starting point, completing a 2.5-mile loop; **Flying Mountain Loop Trail**, an easy to moderately steep, 1.1-mile loop route beginning at the entrance to the Valley Cove, climbing in just .3-mile to the exposed, 284-foot summit of little Flying Mountain, from which are exciting views from above the mouth of Somes Sound, and then descending northward through a spruce forest to the shore of Valley Cove and returning on the Valley Cove Road; **Bernard Peak Loop Trail**, a moderately strenuous, 3.2-mile loop with a few short steep stretches that begins and ends at a parking area on the Western Mountain Road and offers a hike in one of the wildest parts of the park to this 1,071-foot-high summit; **Wonderland Trail**, an easy, .6-mile level pathway beginning at a parking area one mile south of Seawall Campground (on the east side of State Route 102-A), leading through a mixed deciduous-coniferous woodland and a grove of pitch pines, and circling around a small peninsula, on each side of which is a beautiful little cove with pebble beaches, cobblestone seawalls, and granite ledges—a peaceful place to enjoy the sights, sounds, and fragrance of the sea and watch eiders and scoters riding the waves offshore; **Ship Harbor Nature Trail**, an easy, 1.6-mile, self-guided interpretive loop beginning and ending at the Ship Harbor parking area 1.3 miles south of Seawall Campground (on the east side of State Route 102-A); highlights include a view from the head of this sheltered little cove that is nearly drained dry at low tide, a path through a spruce woods, pink-granite ledges at the narrow mouth of the harbor, and frequent opportunities to view eiders, scoters, and other birds. A pamphlet for the Ship Harbor Nature Trail is available at the visitor center or at the Seawall Campground check station.

Boat Cruises

The park sponsors several interpreter-led boat trips to park islands, including:

Schooner Cruise, a three-masted schooner cruise along Acadia's rocky coastline; for information, call 207-288-4585;

Bass Harbor Cruise, a two-hour cruise exploring "Down East" harbors and islands; call 207-244-5365;

Baker Island Cruise, a 4.5-hour cruise to Baker Island; call 207-276-3717;

Islesford Historical Cruise, a three-hour cruise of Somes Sound, with a stop at Islesford Historical Museum on Little Cranberry Island; call 207-276-5352; and

Frenchman Bay Nature Cruise, a two-hour cruise by the islands of Frenchman Bay to view such wildlife as eagles, ospreys, and porpoises; call 207-288-3322.

Cruises for whale-watching, deep-sea fishing, and lobster fishing are available through local charter boat companies. Contact the Bar Harbor Chamber of Commerce for information.

Kayaking

Guided sea-kayaking tours of varying lengths and levels are available, including overnight trips to remote island campsites. Call 207-288-9605 or 800-526-8615 for information.

Swimming

Lifeguards are on duty during the summer at Echo Lake (freshwater) and Sand Beach (saltwater). The Atlantic Ocean is cold, with average temperatures of 55 to 60 degrees Fahrenheit.

Bicycling

The Park Loop Road is open to cyclists, but many prefer the carriage roads that are open. These gravel roadways wind through the eastern half of the island. Cyclists must stay on established roads and are prohibited on trails. Rentals are available in Bar Harbor (207-288-9605). *The Bicycle Guide to Acadia National Park* is available at Hulls Cove Visitor Center. The National Park Service asks that bicyclists follow regulations, wear a helmet, dismount bikes when approaching horses, and thoughtfully signal when approaching hikers from behind.

Horseback Riding and Carriage Rides

Carriage roads are ideal for horseback riding. No horse rentals are available, but stall space and campsites for visiting equestrians are available at Wildwood Stables (207-276-3622). Six carriage rides a day, including a sunset ride to the top of Day Mountain, are

offered between mid-June and Columbus Day in early October. Reservations are strongly recommended. Open carriages are drawn by sturdy Percheron and Belgian draft horses.

Winter Activities

Carriage roads are ideal for cross-country skiing when there is sufficient snow. The Park Loop remains unplowed during the winter and is available for snowmobile use. Ice skating on Acadia's lakes is rarely ideal because of snow, but there may be a brief time in early winter when the lakes and ponds freeze solidly, but before the snow falls. Some of the lakes are popular for ice fishing. Blackwoods Campground is open for winter camping.

Fishing

Freshwater fishing, permitted on all lakes and ponds, requires a state license, available at town offices. Saltwater fishing does not require a license.

OVERNIGHT STAYS

Lodging and Dining

While no lodging is provided within the park, numerous motel, motor inn, and bed-and-breakfast facilities, many open seasonally, are located in such nearby communities as Bar Harbor, Northeast Harbor, and Southwest Harbor. One restaurant, the Jordan Pond House, is located in the park and is open from mid-May to mid-October; reservations are advised for luncheon, afternoon tea-and-popovers, and dinner by calling 207-276-3316. Numerous other restaurants are located on Mount Desert Island, many open seasonally.

Campgrounds

The park provides two fee-charging campgrounds, with a limit of stay of 14 days between mid-May and mid-October and a 30-day limit for the rest of the year. Blackwoods Campground, on the east side of Mount Desert Island, is open year-round, with reservations accepted for the period between mid-June and mid-September by contacting the National

Park Reservation Service at 800-365-CAMP. Sites are available on a first-come, first-served basis the rest of the year. Seawall Campground, near the southern end of the west side of the island, is open from Memorial Day weekend through September on a first-come, first-served basis (group reservations are required).

Backcountry Camping

Backcountry camping is allowed from mid-May to mid-October at Isle au Haut sites. Reservations through park headquarters are required, and a fee is charged. There is a three-day limit of stay between mid-June and mid-September and a five-day limit from mid-May to mid-June and from mid-September to

FLORA AND FAUNA (Partial Listings)

Mammals: whitetail deer, bobcat, red fox, mink, river otter, longtail weasel, porcupine, raccoon, beaver, muskrat, woodchuck, striped skunk, snowshoe hare, squirrels (red, gray, and flying), eastern chipmunk, harbor and gray seals, Atlantic harbor porpoise, and finback, minke, and humpback whales.

Birds: Among the more than 280 species of birds are common loon, pied-billed grebe, double-crested cormorant, great blue heron, mallard, greater scaup, ducks (black, ring-necked, and wood), common goldeneye, buf-flehead, old-squaw, common eider, white-winged scoter, common and red-breasted mer-gansers, hawks (goshawk, sharp-shinned, red-tailed, broad-winged), northern harrier, bald eagle, osprey, peregrine falcon, kestrel, ruffed grouse, black-bellied plover, ruddy turnstone, American woodcock, spotted sandpiper, greater and lesser yellowlegs, sanderling, great black-backed and herring gulls, common and Arctic terns, black guillemot, mourning dove, great horned and barred owls, chimney swift, ruby-throated hummingbird, belted king-fisher, flicker, woodpeckers (pileated, hairy, and downy), eastern kingbird, phoebe, wood pewee, flycatchers (alder, least, great crested, and olive-sided), swallows (tree, barn, and cliff), blue jay, raven, crow, black-capped and boreal chickadees, white-breasted and red-breasted nuthatches, brown creeper, winter wren, catbird, brown thrasher, robin, thrushes (wood, hermit, and Swainson's), veery, gold-en-crowned and ruby-crowned kinglets, cedar waxwing, solitary and red-eyed vireos, war-blers (black-and-white, Tennessee, Nashville, northern parula, yellow, magnolia, black-throated blue, black-throated green, yellow-rumped, palm, blackburnian, chestnut-sided, bay-breasted, blackpoll, Wilson's, and Canada), ovenbird, common yellowthroat, American redstart, red-winged blackbird, scar-let tanager, rose-breasted and evening gros-beaks, indigo bunting, purple finch, American goldfinch, white-winged and red crossbills, rufous-sided towhee, sparrows (savannah,

25

mid-October. Camping is restricted to lean-to shelters provided; no tents are permitted. A pri-vate mail/passenger boat ferries campers to the backcountry camping area from Stonington, Maine. From mid-June through August, the boat lands within 1/10 mile of the camping area; at other times, the boat lands four miles away. It does not run on Sundays or holidays.

sharp-tailed, chipping, white-throated, swamp, and song), and dark-eyed junco.

Reptiles and Amphibians: painted and snapping turtles, snakes (eastern garter, milk, smooth green, red-bellied, and northern ring-neck), spring peeper, frogs (wood, pickerel, and green), bullfrog, and red-backed salamander.

Intertidal Animal Life: acorn barnacle, crumb-of-bread sponge, periwinkle, dog whelk, northern moon shells, Atlantic plate limpet, blue mussel, starfish, brittle star, green sea urchin, sand dollar, sea cucumber, sea anemone, crabs (rock, green, hermit, and Jonah), and soft-shelled, Atlantic razor, little-neck, and longneck clams.

Intertidal Plantlife: corallina, Irish moss, dulse, sea lettuce, knotted rockweed, kelps (horsetail, devil's-apron, winged, and sugar), and bladder wrack (Fucus vesiculosus), F. spiralis, and F. endentatus.

Trees and Shrubs: pines (eastern white, red, jack, and pitch), tamarack (eastern larch), spruces (red, white, and black), eastern hemlock, balsam fir, northern white cedar, quaking and bigtooth aspens, balsam poplar, birches (yellow, paper, and gray), beech, northern red and bear oaks, mountain-ash, shadbush, maples (sugar, red, striped, and mountain), white and black ashes, dwarf and trailing junipers, black crowberry, cranberries (mountain, small, and large), bearberry, rhodora, Labrador tea, sheep and pale laurels, bog rosemary, leatherleaf, huckleberry, lowbush and highbush blueberries, winterberry, mountain-holly, sweetfern, sweetgale, northern bayberry, roses (rugosa, common wild, and swamp), raspberry, blackberry, chokeberry, hobblebush, mapleleaf viburnum, withe rod, red and common elderberries, alternate-leaf dogwood, bush honeysuckle, and staghorn sumac.

Wildflowers: trailing arbutus, goldthread, early saxifrage, starflower, violets (northern white, sweet white, northern blue, and Canada), creeping snowberry, wild lily-of-the-valley, twisted stalk, clintonia, Solomon's and false Solomon's seals, bunchberry, pink lady's-slipper, wintergreen, partridgeberry, wood sorrel, shinleaf, round-leaved pyrola, rattlesnake plantain, wild sarsaparilla, Indian pipe, beech-drops, wine-leaved cinquefoil, golden-heather, mountain sandwort, wood lily, harebell, baked-apple berry, arethusa, calopogon, rose pogonia, pitcher-plant, round-leaved sundew, iris, purple-fringed orchis, skunk cabbage, cat-tail, water lily, spatterdock, narrow-leaved arrowhead, pickerelweed, common bladder-wort, water lobelia, cardinal flower, bluet, blue-eyed grass, lupine, evening primrose, black-eyed susan, oxeye daisy, meadowsweet, steeplebush, fireweed, St. Johnswort, Canada thistle, goldenrods (early, Canada, gray, seaside, and lance-leaved), asters (flat-topped, New England, whorled wood, and big-leaved), beach pea, silver-and-gold, hedge bindweed, and sea-lavender.

Ferns: bracken, common polypody, rusty woodsia, Christmas, crested shield, marginal and spinulose wood, lady, cinnamon, narrow beech, oak, sensitive, royal, interrupted, New York, and hayscented ferns.

NEARBY POINTS OF INTEREST

The area surrounding the park offers many other exciting natural and historical attractions that can be enjoyed as day trips or overnight excursions. Farther "down east" are Petit Manan and Moosehorn national wildlife refuges, Quoddy Head State Park, Saint Croix Island International Historic Site, and Roosevelt Campobello International Park, the latter on Canada's Campobello Island. To the north are Baxter State Park and the Allagash Wilderness Waterway.

APPALACHIAN NATIONAL SCENIC TRAIL

▲ Near the summit of Hawksbill Mountain

Appalachian National Scenic Trail

P.O. Box 807
Harpers Ferry, WV 25425-0807
304-535-6331

This 2,146-mile-long, 172,109-acre national scenic trail runs from Mount Katahdin, in Baxter State Park, Maine; southwestward through the White Mountains of New Hampshire, the Green Mountains of Vermont, and the Berkshire Hills of western Massachusetts; along ridges of the Appalachian Mountains, including Shenandoah National Park, Virginia, and Great Smoky Mountains National Park, Tennessee-North Carolina; and ending on Springer Mountain, Georgia. The Appalachian Trail was begun in the mid-1920s to protect an accessible wilderness belt for hiking and has since been designed, constructed, marked, and maintained by volunteer hiking clubs, joined together by the nonprofit Appalachian Trail Conference (ATC), and supported by active partners, such as the National Park Service, U.S. Forest Service, state parks and forests, and local communities. In 1968, the trail corridor was established as a national scenic trail.

OUTSTANDING FEATURES

Among the many outstanding features of the trail are the following:

In Maine: isolated regions of mountains, lakes, ponds, streams, and wild forests; rugged climbs, such as 5,268-foot Mount Katahdin (northern terminus of the trail), 4,150-foot Bigelow Mountain above Flagstaff Lake, and 4,116-foot Saddleback Mountain near the Rangeley Lakes in western Maine; opportunities for canoeing and swimming; and the magnificent color of autumn foliage from mid-September to early October.

In New Hampshire: the rugged White Mountains of the White Mountain National Forest, including 6,288-foot Mount

Washington; alternating mountains and valleys; and the Connecticut River.

In Vermont: a rolling countryside of woodlands, with abandoned and overgrown farmlands; and a stretch of the Green Mountains, in the scenic southern part of the Green Mountain National Forest.

In Massachusetts: gently rolling, forested mountains in the Berkshire Hills, including 3,491-foot Mount Greylock.

In Connecticut: gently rolling hills of the Taconic Range and the scenic Housatonic River valley.

In New York: farming country, the Hudson River, and Bear Mountain and Harriman state parks.

In New Jersey: the rugged ridge of the Kittatinny Mountains, High Point State Park, Stokes State Forest, and the Delaware Water Gap National Recreation Area.

In Pennsylvania: the rim of the eastern range of the Alleghenies, the Susquehanna River, Cumberland Valley, and the northernmost extension of the Blue Ridge Mountains.

In Maryland: the ridge crest of South Mountain, the Chesapeake & Ohio Canal towpath, and the Potomac River.

In West Virginia: Harpers Ferry National Historical Park, ATC headquarters in Harpers Ferry, and the Shenandoah River.

In Virginia: extraordinary views along the crest of the Blue Ridge Mountains in Shenandoah National Park and the Jefferson National Forest; and autumn foliage in October.

In Tennessee and North Carolina: Appalachian ranges in the Cherokee and Pisgah national forests; Great Smoky Mountains National Park, including 6,643-foot Clingmans Dome; Nantahala National Forest, including 5,498-foot Standing Indian Mountain, known as the "Grandstand of the Southern Appalachians"; floral displays of rhododendrons and mountain laurel in June and July; and magnificent autumn foliage in October.

In Georgia: Chattahoochee National Forest, with its wild mountain beauty; and the southern terminus of the trail on 1,153-foot Springer Mountain.

▲ *The Blue Ridge Mountains, Virginia*

PRACTICAL INFORMATION

When to Go

Most through-hikers start their trips on Springer Mountain, Georgia, in April and finish on Mount Katahdin, Maine, in September. Inclement weather is more likely in early April, so a mid-month start is advisable. Maine's Baxter State Park is closed October 15-May 15, and the trail to the summit of Mount Katahdin is closed whenever the weather makes hiking dangerous. Drastic weather changes, summer thunderstorms, and off-season cold weather are all common throughout this region.

Fees and Permits

Permits to walk the trail or its side trails in the Great Smoky Mountains are not required, but permits for overnight use in Great Smoky Mountains National Park, Shenandoah National Park, and parts of the White Mountain National Forest are required. They are free and available at park or forest ranger stations. Contact those locations or the ATC for detailed information. A $2 users fee is charged in Harpers Ferry National Historical Park for hikers who leave the trail to visit exhibits, shops, and other attractions in the park district. Baxter State Park has strict limits on the number of visitors and will close the gates once campgrounds are full; contact the park for information and regulations.

Entrances

Of the more than 500 entrances to the trail, the initial northern entrance is at Katahdin, Maine, and the initial southern entrance is at Springer Mountain, Georgia. Guidebooks, maps, and other publications may be obtained from the ATC.

Headquarters

ATC Headquarters is located near the halfway point in Harpers Ferry, West Virginia. The site offers trail and ATC membership information, guidebooks, maps, publications, volunteer information, a log book, trail history, and photos of through-hikers.

Facilities

Facilities vary along the trail, but many areas are close to towns. Volunteers have built and maintain more than 250 three-sided shelters located along the trail for use by all hikers. There are eight three-sided huts in Shenandoah National Park and a full-service hut system, tent platforms, and shelters in the White Mountains of New Hampshire for use by long-distance hikers. Trail markers are visible all along the trail and are denoted by white-paint blazes two inches wide and six inches high on trees, poles, or rocks. Blazes in blue paint indicate side trails to water, viewpoints, and shelters.

Handicapped Accessibility

The trail has been hiked by many individuals with various disabilities including the visually and mobility-impaired, although there are no specific access provisions other than at developed campsites.

Medical Services

First aid, hospitals, and other medical services are available in towns along the trail.

Pets

Horses and pack animals are not permitted on the Appalachian Trial, except at one location in the Smokies and at a few crossings by designated horse trails. Dogs are not permitted in Great Smoky Mountains National Park and Baxter State Park and must be leashed at all times in Shenandoah National Park. It is recommended that you leave pets at home to avoid unpleasant encounters with wildlife and other hikers.

Safety and Regulations

While generally safe, the trail is not immune to crime or hazards. Some basic points are:

- Do not hike alone. Leave a trip itinerary with family and friends, but avoid broadcasting it to strangers or other hikers.

- Dress conservatively so as not to attract unwelcome attention, but wear blaze-orange attire during hunting season.

- Avoid provocation. Camp away from roads, and don't carry firearms.

- Don't leave your pack unattended.

- Report any incidents of harassment to local law enforcement authorities and to the ATC.

Lodgings

The 250 three-sided shelters located along the trail are for use by all hikers. They are spaced at least ten miles apart, and in many areas camping is not permitted between shelters. Hikers are urged to keep the shelter grounds litter free, not to cut down trees or vandalize the shelters, and always to practice minimum-impact camping.

For more comfortable accommodations, consult the trail Data Book, available through the ATC, which lists hostels and other types of nearby accommodations.

ASSATEAGUE ISLAND NATIONAL SEASHORE

▲ Algae pools and marsh grass

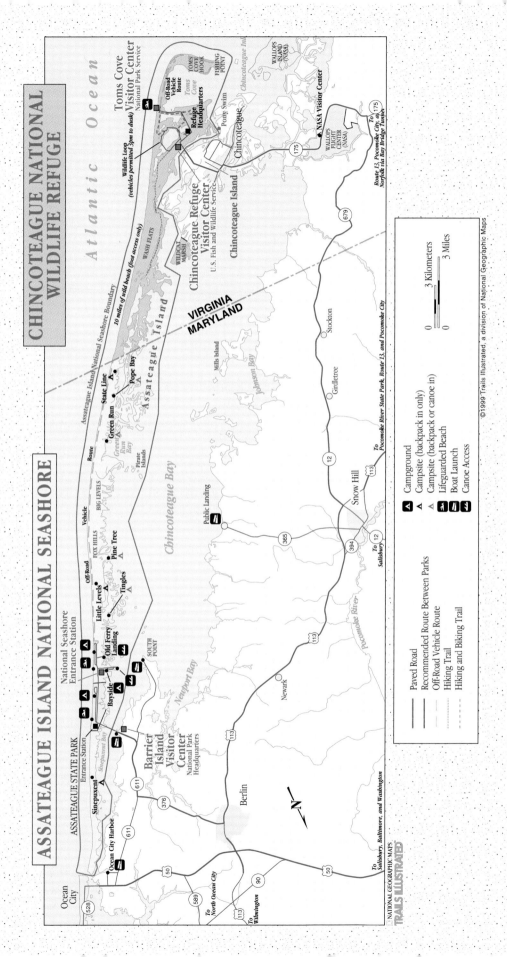

ASSATEAGUE ISLAND NATIONAL SEASHORE

CHINCOTEAGUE NATIONAL WILDLIFE REFUGE

NATIONAL GEOGRAPHIC MAPS
TRAILS ILLUSTRATED

©1999 Trails Illustrated, a division of National Geographic Maps

Legend:
- Paved Road
- Recommended Route Between Parks
- Off-Road Vehicle Route
- Hiking Trail
- Hiking and Biking Trail
- Campground
- Campsite (backpack in only)
- Campsite (backpack or canoe in)
- Lifeguarded Beach
- Boat Launch
- Canoe Access

3 Kilometers
3 Miles
0   3

VIRGINIA
MARYLAND

Atlantic Ocean

ASSATEAGUE ISLAND NATIONAL SEASHORE

7206 National Seashore Lane
Berlin, MD 21811-9742
410-641-1441

This 39,721-acre national seashore, along the Atlantic shore of Maryland and Virginia, protects a 37-mile-long barrier island that consists of outer sand beaches, sand dunes, areas of loblolly pine woodlands, and saltmarsh habitat along the island's inner shore. The seashore is an outstanding area for birdwatching, notably of shorebirds and migratory waterfowl. Two herds of wild ponies also roam the island. With the numbers of these animals steadily increasing in recent years, their impact on dune and marsh ecosystems has become harmful, so the National Park Service has begun implementing a birth-control program among their population.

Chincoteague National Wildlife Refuge and Maryland's Assateague State Park are also within the national seashore, which was established in 1965.

ACTIVITIES

Options include swimming, surfing, hiking, birdwatching, interpretive programs, bicycling, canoeing, boating, boat tours, camping, picnicking, shell-collecting, surf fishing, crabbing, clamming, off-road vehicle driving in some places, wild-pony viewing, pony round-up and auction, and public hunting in part of the seashore during the designated season. Further information is available in the park's newspaper, *Assateague Island—A Visitor Guide*.

PRACTICAL INFORMATION

When to Go

The Maryland portion of the seashore is open year-round, but overnight stays are permitted only in designated campgrounds or backcountry sites or for visitors who are surf fishing. The national wildlife refuge is open year-round. The annual pony penning and auction event occurs on the last Wednesday and Thursday of July. Poison ivy, ticks, and mosquitoes are abundant on the seashore from spring through autumn.

How to Get There

By Car: In Maryland, take U.S. Route 50 east from Salisbury and drive south on MD Route 611 to the Barrier Island Visitor Center and the bridge to the island. In Virginia, from U.S. Route 13, drive east on VA Route 175 through the town of Chincoteague and into the national wildlife refuge.

By Air: Baltimore-Washington International Airport (410-859-7111) and Ocean City Regional Airport (410-213-2471) are served by a number of airlines.

By Train: Amtrak (800-872-7245) has stops in Baltimore, Maryland, and Norfolk, Virginia.

By Bus: Greyhound Lines (800-231-2222) has stops in Ocean City.

Fees and Permits

Entrance fees are $5 per vehicle and are valid for seven consecutive days. Backcountry-use permits are required and must be obtained by mid-afternoon from park offices. Off-road vehicles require permits, which are available for a fee at park offices during normal business hours or by mail. Vehicle specifications and equipment regulations are strictly enforced. After hours, surf fishing in Virginia is allowed by special permit; no permit is necessary in Maryland. Permits are required for archery and firearm hunting.

Visitor Centers

Barrier Island Visitor Center (410-641-1441), in Maryland. Interpretive exhibits and publications.

Tom's Cove Visitor Center (804-336-6577), in Virginia (National Park Service). Interpretive exhibits and publications.

Chincoteague Refuge Visitor Center (804-336-6122), in Virginia (U.S. Fish and Wildlife Service). Information, descriptive brochures, schedules of wildlife tours, and other interpretive activities.

Facilities

Available are picnic areas, campgrounds, backcountry camp sites, bathhouses, rinse-off showers, rest facilities, drinking water, trails, canoe and bicycle rentals, and boat ramp. The state park offers a picnic area, a campground, hot showers, rest facilities, dump stations, and a small campstore and restaurant during the summer.

Handicapped Accessibility

Visitor centers, bath houses, and some nature trails and campsites are wheelchair accessible. Campsites must be reserved in advance.

Medical Services

Emergency first aid is available and administered by qualified national seashore staff in the Maryland and Virginia portions of Assateague. Hospitals are in Berlin, Maryland, eight miles from the Maryland entrance, and in Salisbury, Maryland, 45 miles from the Virginia entrance.

Pets

Pets are prohibited in Chincoteague National Wildlife Refuge, Assateague State Park, the primitive area north of the state park, and all backcountry campsites. In the Maryland end of the national seashore, they are permitted, but must be on leashes no longer than six feet. However, visitors are advised to leave pets at home because blowing sand and salt spray are hard on the eyes and feet of dogs, and pests like heartworms and ticks can further endanger their health.

Safety and Regulations

For your safety and enjoyment and for the protection of the park, please follow these regulations and suggestions:

- Visitors are cautioned not to approach, feed, or pet wild ponies as these wild animals are prone to unpredictable behavior and may kick or bite.

- Off-road vehicles must stay on marked

beach vehicle routes and away from all sand dunes and vegetated areas.

- Swimmers should use only the life-guarded beaches for water activities and be careful of breaking surf.

- Guard against ticks, mosquitoes, and poison ivy, all prevalent from spring through autumn.

▲ *The beachfront at Assateague Island National Seashore, Maryland*

OVERNIGHT STAYS

Lodging and Dining

There are no lodging or dining facilities in the seashore. The nearby communities of Ocean City, Maryland, and Chincoteague, Virginia, provide a wide variety of accommodations and restaurants.

Campgrounds

Sites are available on a first-come, first-served basis from November 1 to May 15 and by reservation from May 15 to October 15 by contacting the National Park Reservation Service at 800-365-CAMP.

In Maryland, two campgrounds are provided, Oceanside and Bayside, which accommodate any size camping unit (dump station only, no hookups) and have primitive outdoor facilities. Oceanside has several sites for tents only. From May through September, there is a seven-day limit of stay; in the rest of the year, there is a 30-day limit. Group camping for 12 to 25 persons is offered year-round by reservation. The state park also provides a campground.

In Virginia, no camping is allowed in the national wildlife refuge, but commercial campgrounds are available on adjacent Chincoteague Island.

Campgrounds are usually full every day from mid-June to Labor Day and on weekends through the spring and autumn. None of the developed campsites is shaded. Tent campers should bring 18-inch-long stakes for camping in sandy soil and occasional strong winds.

Backcountry Camping

Backcountry camping is allowed at designated sites on a first-come, first-served basis with free permits. There are four bayside backcountry sites (hike-in or boat-in) and three ocean-side sites (hike-in) available year-round, except for the week of firearms deer season in late November. In summer, campers may be discouraged from using bayside sites because of biting insects. Sites include a chemical toilet and picnic table, but no drinking water. The nearest ocean-side camp is four miles from parking.

FLORA AND FAUNA (Partial Listings)

Mammals: whitetail and Sika deer, feral horse (wild pony), red fox, river otter, longtail weasel, opossum, raccoon, muskrat, eastern cottontail, Delmarva Peninsula fox squirrel (endangered species), eastern chipmunk, gray seal, and bottle-nose dolphin.

Birds: mute and tundra (whistling) swans, Canada and snow geese, brant, black duck, gadwall, pintail, wood duck, mallard, blue-winged and green-winged teal, American wigeon, ring-necked duck, lesser and greater scaups, ruddy duck, hooded merganser, coot, common gallinule, brown pelican, gulls (herring, ring-billed, great black-backed, and laughing), terns (royal, Caspian, little [least], common, and Forster's), herons (great blue, little blue, green-backed, and Louisiana), black-crowned night-heron, egrets (great, snowy, and cattle), least and American bitterns, glossy ibis, rails (Virginia, king, clapper, sora, and black), American oystercatcher, plovers (black-bellied, Wilson's, and piping), killdeer, woodcock, willet, greater and lesser yellowlegs, sanderling, dunlin, sandpipers (purple, spotted, western, and least), bald eagle, osprey, peregrine falcon, chuck-will's widow, nighthawk, belted kingfisher, yellow-bellied sapsucker, eastern kingbird, eastern wood pewee, tree swallow, Carolina chickadee, tufted titmouse, white-breasted and brown-headed nuthatches, wrens (house, marsh, sedge, and Carolina), blue-gray gnatcatcher, brown thrasher, catbird, robin, red-eyed and white-eyed vireos, American redstart, warblers (pine, prairie, and yellow), common yellowthroat, northern waterthrush, red-winged blackbird, cardinal, American goldfinch, indigo bunting, rufous-sided towhee, and field, song, savannah, sharp-tailed, and seaside sparrows.

Trees, Shrubs, and Flowers: loblolly pine, sassafras, southern red oak, American holly, red maple, wax myrtle, bayberry, greenbrier, and muscadine grape.

NEARBY POINTS OF INTEREST

The area surrounding this seashore offers many significant natural and historical attractions that can be enjoyed as day trips or overnight excursions. East of Chesapeake Bay, in eastern Maryland, are Blackwater and Eastern Neck Island national wildlife refuges. To the north, in Delaware, are Prime Hook and Bombay Hook national wildlife refuges. To the southwest, in Virginia, are Colonial National Historical Park, Richmond National Battlefield Park, and Petersburg National Battlefield. Numerous National Capital Parks are located in Washington, D.C. Fort Washington Park, Piscataway Park, and Thomas Stone National Historic Site are in southern Maryland. The Ward Museum of Wildfowl Art is located in Salisbury, Maryland.

CAPE COD NATIONAL SEASHORE

▲ *Beach grasses and sand dunes*

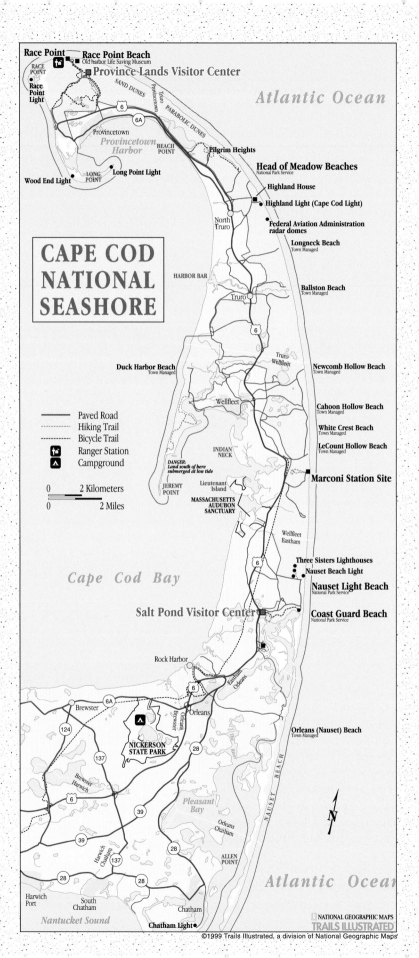

CAPE COD NATIONAL SEASHORE

Race Point
Race Point Beach
Old harbor Life Saving Museum
Province Lands Visitor Center

RACE POINT

Race Point Light

Atlantic Ocean

SAND DUNES

6

6A

Provincetown

PARABOLIC DUNES

Provincetown Harbor

BEACH POINT

Pilgrim Heights

Wood End Light

LONG POINT

Long Point Light

Head of Meadow Beaches
National Park Service

Highland House

North Truro

Highland Light (Cape Cod Light)

Federal Aviation Administration radar domes

Longneck Beach
Town Managed

HARBOR BAR

Truro

Ballston Beach
Town Managed

6

Truro
Wellfleet

Newcomb Hollow Beach
Town Managed

Duck Harbor Beach
Town Managed

Wellfleet

Cahoon Hollow Beach
Town Managed

White Crest Beach
Town Managed

INDIAN NECK

LeCount Hollow Beach
Town Managed

DANGER:
Land south of here submerged at low tide

JEREMY POINT

Lieutenant Island

Marconi Station Site

MASSACHUSETTS AUDUBON SANCTUARY

Wellfleet
Eastham

Three Sisters Lighthouses
Nauset Beach Light

6

Nauset Light Beach
National Park Service

Cape Cod Bay

Salt Pond Visitor Center

Coast Guard Beach
National Park Service

Rock Harbor

6

Eastham
Orleans

Brewster

6A

Orleans

Brewster

Orleans (Nauset) Beach
Town Managed

124

137

NICKERSON STATE PARK

28

Brewster
Harwich

6

Pleasant Bay

39

39

Orleans
Chatham

ALLEN POINT

39

137

28

28

28

Atlantic Ocean

Harwich Port

South Chatham

Chatham

Chatham Light

Nantucket Sound

NAUSET BEACH

N

— Paved Road
---- Hiking Trail
--- Bicycle Trail
🏠 Ranger Station
⛺ Campground

0   2 Kilometers
0   2 Miles

38

Cape Cod National Seashore

99 Marconi Site Road
Wellfleet, MA 02667
508-349-3785

Established in 1961, this 43,569-acre national seashore in eastern Massachusetts protects a beautiful, 40-mile stretch of Cape Cod, including Atlantic Ocean beaches, bluffs, sand dunes, kettle ponds, saltmarsh, white cedar swamp, and pitch pine and bear oak woodlands. Cape Cod is largely the creation of continental glaciation 15,000 to 20,000 years ago, during the Pleistocene Epoch (the most recent Ice Age). It consists of huge quantities of rocks and other sediments deposited at the margins of the glacier, forming a large end moraine (ridge) and massive outwash fans. The ocean and wind are constantly changing the cape's shorelines, tearing away in one area and rebuilding in another.

Cape Cod is also rich in human history, including the Pilgrims' landing in 1620, fishing and whaling, and clamming and cranberry harvesting. And it is a place that has long attracted vacationers, artists, and writers, some of whom have written about the area. Examples include Henry Beston's The *Outermost House: A Year of Life on the Great Beach of Cape Cod* (1929) and Henry David Thoreau's *Cape Cod* (1864).

OUTSTANDING FEATURES

Among the many outstanding features of the seashore are the following: **Old Harbor Lifesaving Station**, which was moved in two pieces from Chatham to Race Point in 1977; **Provincetown**, a village adjacent to the national seashore where the Pilgrims landed in 1620; **Great Island**, an area once separate from Cape Cod where whalers used to congregate; **Nauset Light**, one of five lighthouses within the seashore; **Penniman House**, the ornate 1868 Eastham home of prominent whaler Captain Edward Penniman; and the **Atwood-Higgins House**, a typical Cape Cod dwelling dating from around 1730.

PRACTICAL INFORMATION

When to Go

The seashore is open daily. The climate is notably milder than inland, since the cape extends about 30 miles out from the mainland toward the warm Gulf Stream. Summers are cooler and winters are milder than the rest of the state.

How to Get There

By Car: Take U.S. Route 6 east onto Cape Cod, then 40 miles to Orleans and north 27 miles, adjacent to and through the national seashore. The route ends at Provincetown.

By Air: Barnstable Municipal Airport is served by several airlines and Provincetown Municipal Airport is served by Cape Air. International airports are located in Boston and New York.

By Train: Amtrak (800-872-7245) may offer limited summer service to Hyannis.

By Bus: Greyhound Lines (800-231-2222) has stops throughout the park.

Fees and Permits

Entrance fees are $7 per car per day at the seashore's six beaches or $1 per day for persons bicycling or walking to the beaches. A seasonal pass is available for $20. State licenses are required for freshwater fishing, but not for saltwater fishing. Town licenses are required for shellfishing. Federal, state, and local laws apply to public hunting. Permits, available at visitor centers, are required for open fires. Off road vehicle permits are required and available at Race Point Ranger Station in Provincetown.

Visitor Centers

Salt Pond Visitor Center, in Eastham, and Province Lands Visitor Center, just north of Provincetown: both are open daily from mid-April to December. Interpretive exhibits, audiovisual programs, and publications.

Facilities

Beach facilities are available, as are picnic areas and summer shuttle-bus service.

40

▲ *Highland Light at Cape Cod National Seashore, Massachusetts*

Handicapped Accessibility

Parking lots, restrooms, visitor centers, headquarters, Coast Guard Beach, Herring Cove Beach, and Marconi Station and Fort Hill overlooks are wheelchair-accessible. The Buttonbush Trail for the Blind is in Eastham. Contact park headquarters for a detailed accessibility guide.

Medical Services

Emergency first aid only is available in the national seashore. Medical services are available in nearby communities. A hospital is located in Hyannis, 30 miles away.

Pets

Pets must be kept under physical restraint, and leashes must not exceed six feet. Pets are prohibited in public buildings, in picnic areas, and on trails and protected beaches.

Safety and Regulations

For your safety and enjoyment and for the protection of the park, please follow these regulations and suggestions:

- Climbing slopes or digging deep holes in the sand is potentially hazardous.

- Swim only where lifeguards are on duty. Swimmers are cautioned to be alert for riptides and underwater obstacles.

- Surfing and boardsailing are permitted in waters outside lifeguarded beaches.

- Regulations prohibit taking glass containers, rafts, rubber tubes, snorkels, and masks to any beach.

- The use of motorized vehicles, including mopeds, are prohibited on bicycle trails.

- Upland game and migratory waterfowl may be hunted in certain areas during the designated season (there is no open season on non-game species).

- Visitors are cautioned to be alert for ticks, especially as they may carry the bacteria that causes Lyme disease.

ACTIVITIES

Options include swimming, hiking, birdwatching, interpretive walks and talks, bicycling, canoeing, horseback riding, picnicking, surfing and windsurfing, beach vehicle driving, shellfishing, fishing, and public hunting in part of the seashore during the designated season. Further information is available in the park's newspaper, *The Cape Cod Guide*.

Hiking

A number of short hiking trails lead through or to points of special interest. Among them are the one-mile **Beech Forest Trail**, near Provincetown; the .75-mile **Pilgrim Spring** and the .75-mile **Small Swamp trails** at Pilgrim Heights; the half-mile **Pamet Cranberry Bog Trail**, near the Environmental Education Center at Ballston Beach on Truro; the 1.25-mile **Atlantic White Cedar Swamp Trail**, near the historic Marconi Station Site; in Wellfleet and the one-mile **Nauset Marsh**, half-mile **Red Maple Swamp**, and 1.5-mile **Fort Hill trails**, near Eastham.

On **Great Island**, a three-mile one-way trail leads to Jeremy Point Overlook (an eight-mile round-trip, via the Tavern Site route). Hikers on the Great Island trails are cautioned to check tides in advance.

Bicycling

A five-mile network of bicycle trails leads from the Province Lands Visitor Center, north of Provincetown; the two-mile Head of the Meadow Trail passes through Pilgrim Heights, between Head of the Meadow and High Head roads; and the popular Cape Cod Rail Trail runs from Nickerson State Park, goes near the Salt Pond Visitor Center, and connects with the 1.6-mile Nauset Trail that runs out to Coast Guard Beach.

OVERNIGHT STAYS

Lodging and Dining

There are no lodging or dining facilities within the seashore. Nearby communities provide many lodging and camping accommodations, restaurants, gift shops, grocery and other stores, and service stations. Advance reservations at motels, hotels, and private campgrounds are essential in the summer.

Campgrounds

While there are no campgrounds administered by the national seashore, Nickerson State Park (which is reached on State Route 6A nearby in Brewster) provides camping on a first-come, first-served basis.

Backcountry Camping

All camping, including trailers on the beach, is prohibited, except in private campgrounds outside the national seashore.

FLORA AND FAUNA (Partial Listings)

Mammals: whitetail deer, red fox, river otter, raccoon, opossum, woodchuck, muskrat, striped skunk, eastern cottontail, squirrels (eastern gray, red, and flying), eastern chipmunk, harbor and gray seals, Atlantic white-sided dolphin, and pilot whale.

Birds: Canada goose, black and wood ducks, mallard, scoters (white-winged, surf, and black), common eider, greater scaup, ruddy duck, red-breasted merganser, bufflehead, gulls (ring-billed, herring, and great black-backed), terns (Arctic, common, little [least], and roseate), great blue and green-backed herons, black-crowned night-heron, Virginia rail, piping plover, killdeer, spotted sandpiper, bobwhite, northern harrier, kestrel, great horned owl, mourning dove, ruby-throated hummingbird, belted kingfisher, downy wood-pecker, flicker, horned lark, eastern kingbird, great crested flycatcher, eastern phoebe, eastern wood pewee, swallows (barn, tree, and bank), crow, blue jay, black-capped chickadee, tufted titmouse, white-breasted and red-breasted nuthatches, Carolina and marsh wrens, brown thrasher, catbird, mockingbird, eastern bluebird, robin, red-eyed vireo, warblers (black-and-white, pine, prairie, yellow-rumped, and yellow), American redstart, common yellowthroat, ovenbird, red-winged blackbird, eastern meadowlark, cardinal, house and purple finches, American goldfinch, rufous-sided towhee, and chipping, song, savannah, and sharp-tailed sparrows.

Trees, Shrubs, Flowers, and Grasses: pitch pine, Atlantic white cedar, eastern redcedar, sassafras, black gum, beech, oaks (white, bear, and black), black cherry, red maple, beach plum, shadbush, buttonbush, bayberry, highbush and lowbush blueberries, sheep laurel, swamp azalea, American cranberry, rugosa rose, crowberry, golden-heather, sweetfern, seaside lavender, beach pea, starflower, mayflower, glasswort, American beach grass, salt meadow grass, and salt-marsh cordgrass.

NEARBY POINTS OF INTEREST

The area surrounding the seashore offers many exciting attractions that can be enjoyed as day trips or overnight excursions. Manuel F. Corellus State Forest is located on nearby Martha's Vineyard, and Shawme-Crowell and Myles Standish state forests are located inland near Plymouth. A dozen other National Park System units are located throughout the state, many of them centered around Boston.

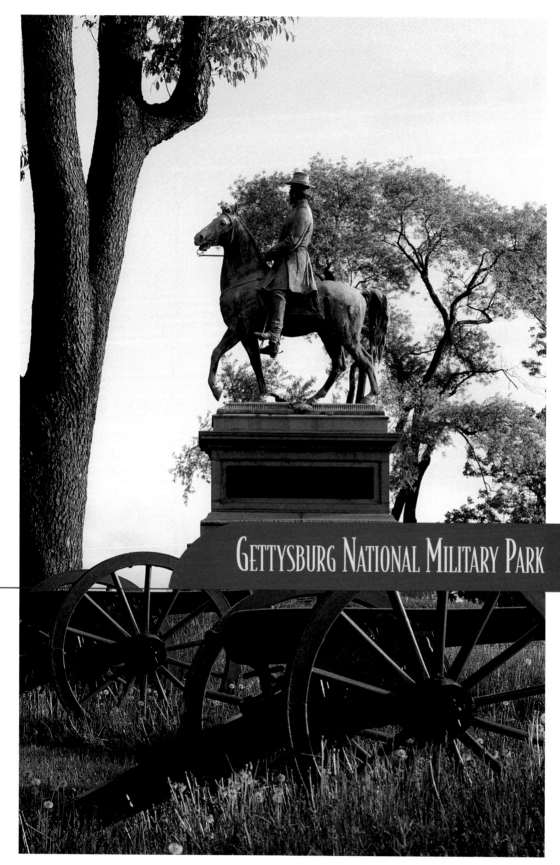

▲ *Cemetery Hill*

GETTYSBURG NATIONAL MILITARY PARK

Mummasburg Rd

Carlisle Rd

BR 15

Hanoverburg Rd

To Chambersburg

Western Maryland Railroad

Chambersburg Pike

Eternal Light Peace Memorial

BARLOW KNOLL

York Pike

Oak Ridge

Observation Tower

34

Buford Ave

Doubleday Ave

Howard Ave

Rock Creek

To East Cavalry Battlefield Site Entrance

The Railroad Cut

Lincoln St

Gettysburg College

Washington St

Carlisle St

Stratton St

GETTYSBURG

McPherson Ridge

Seminary Ave

Stevens Run

York St

East Middle St

Baltimore St

East Confederate Ave

Hanover Rd

Lutheran Theological Seminary

BRENNER'S HILL

Hagerstown Rd

116

Youth Group Campground

McMILLAN WOODS

Gettysburg Hospital

Visitors Center

National Cemetery
Soldiers National Monument

Observation Tower

CULP'S HILL

North Carolina Memorial

Cyclorama Center

Spangler's Spring

High Water Mark

Meade's Headquarters

Hunt Ave

West Confederate Ave

Virginia Memorial

Copse of Trees

Taneytown Rd

Amphitheatre

Pennsylvania Memorial

Granite School House Lane

97

Baltimore Pike

Pitzer Woods

Sickles Ave

Black Horse Tavern Rd

The Peach Orchard

United States Ave

States Ave

Wheatfield Rd

Plum Run
The Wheatfield

Pumping Station Rd

Millerstown Rd

Observation Tower

Rose Farm

Red Rock Rd

EISENHOWER
NATIONAL
HISTORIC
SITE

Devil's Den

Little Round Top

15

South Confederate Ave

Warfield Ridge

Big Round Top Loop Trail

Wright Ave

Big Round Top

Emmitsburg Rd

SOUTH CAVALRY FIELD

BR 15

134

To Interstate 70, Interstate 270, and Washington, D.C.

—— Auto Tour

‑ ‑ ‑ Culp's Hill Auto Tour

········ Hiking Trail

0   1 Kilometer

0   1 Mile

44

Gettysburg National Military Park

97 Taneytown Road
Gettysburg, PA 17325-1080
717-334-1124

Established in 1895, this 5,906-acre national military park in southern Pennsylvania protects and interprets the site of the Civil War's fiercely fought Battle of Gettysburg on July 1-3, 1863, in which the Union army decisively defeated the Confederates in their second invasion of the North. There were more casualties in this three-day combat than in any other battle before or since fought in North America.

In June, Confederate General Robert E. Lee's 70,000-man Army of Northern Virginia confidently crossed the Potomac River into the North, where they encountered the 93,000-man Union army led by their recently appointed commander, Major General George G. Meade. The two armies first clashed just to the north and west of the town of Gettysburg, resulting in heavy casualties on both sides, and the Confederates succeeded in driving the Northerners back through and around town. But by the end of the first day and into that night, Union troops, with a steady flow of reinforcements, were establishing strong defensive positions on the hills south of town—notably on Cemetery Hill and Culp's Hill and along Cemetery Ridge.

On the afternoon of the second day, one of the fierce and bloody clashes erupted over control of a rocky promontory known as Little Round Top. As the Southerners attempted to reach this high ground, the Union defenders unleashed a hail of gunfire. Below the summit, savage hand-to-hand combat raged in a boulder-jumbled area called Devil's Den and in a marshy place that came to be known as the "Valley of Death." A Union officer who witnessed this awesome spectacle described it as "full of smoke and fire, and literally swarming with riderless horses and fighting, fleeing and pursuing men. The wild cries of charging lines, the rattle of musketry, the booming of artillery and the shrieks of the wounded were the orchestral accompaniments of a scene like very hell itself." By that evening, the Confederates were in retreat.

On the afternoon of the third day, the Confederates first launched a massive, two-hour artillery bombardment of Cemetery Ridge; then their infantry units began a major frontal assault, later referred to as Pickett's Charge. As the Southerners roared eastward across the gently rolling fields, they were mowed down like wheat by a huge scythe, as Union cannon and muskets unleashed a flaming blizzard of lead and iron. Of the 12,000 Confederate soldiers who surged into the Union volleys, 7,000 were killed, wounded, or captured. On the next day, the remaining Southerners began their retreat back to Virginia—thus ending the Pennsylvania Campaign. In the three-day conflict, the Confederates sustained more than 28,000 casualties, and the Union army lost 23,000 fighting men.

After this devastating battle, the state of Pennsylvania commissioned the establishment of a national cemetery. In the dedication ceremony, on November 19, 1863, President Abraham Lincoln delivered his famous Gettysburg Address. That speech, a masterpiece of eloquence, helped transform Gettysburg from a scene of carnage to a symbol that continues to give meaning to the dead and inspiration to the living. As President Lincoln said, "It is for us the living . . . to be here dedicated to the great task remaining before us—that from these honored dead we take increased devotion to that cause for which they gave the last full measure of devotion . . . —that this nation, under God, shall have a new birth of freedom—and that government of the people, by the people, for the people, shall not perish from the earth."

OUTSTANDING FEATURES

Among the many outstanding features of the park are the following: **Meade's Headquarters**, the modest little house where the Union commander made many battle decisions; such **major military sites** as The Angle, Cemetery Ridge, Little Round Top, Devil's Den, The Wheatfield, The Peach

Orchard, Pitzer Woods, Seminary Ridge, Culp's Hill, and Cemetery Hill; **High Water Mark Trail**, featuring regimental monuments, part of an artillery battery, the ground defended by Union soldiers, and Meade's headquarters; **Big Round Top Loop Trail**, revealing some of the hardwood forest's typical fauna and flora and stone military breastworks built by the armies; and the **National Cemetery**, adjacent to the park, where President Lincoln delivered his Gettysburg Address and the final resting place for more than 7,000 servicemen and their dependents.

PRACTICAL INFORMATION

When to Go

The park is open year-round.

How to Get There

By Car: A variety of routes converge at Gettysburg, including U.S. Route 30, between I-83 at York and I-81 at Chambersburg, and U.S. Route 15, between the Pennsylvania Turnpike (I-76) at Harrisburg and I-70 at

licensed battlefield guides, are offered for groups; contact the park for reservations.

Fees and Permits

The fee for viewing the electric map and the Cyclorama Center is $3 for adults, $2.50 for seniors, and $1.50 for youth aged 6-16.

Visitor Center and Museums

Visitor Center and Gettysburg Museum of the Civil War: open daily, except for Thanksgiving, Christmas, and New Year's Day. Orientation displays, Civil War exhibits, current schedules of ranger-conducted programs, and the electric map presentation that shows troop movements during the battle.

Cyclorama Center: open daily. Exhibits, a film, and the Gettysburg Cyclorama painting featuring a sound-and-light program.

Facilities

Included are picnic facilities and an amphitheater.

Handicapped Accessibility

Visitor center and Cyclorama Center restrooms and major program areas are wheelchair-accessible. Brochures and audiotapes with players are available for the visually and hearing impaired. The orientation film, *Gettysburg 1863*, is captioned.

Medical Services

Emergency first aid is available in the park. A hospital is located in the town of Gettysburg.

Pets

Pets must be leashed and attended at all times. They are prohibited in the visitor center, Cyclorama Center, and the National Cemetery.

Safety and Regulations

All historic sites, structures, and exhibits, as well as plants, animals, and minerals, must be left undisturbed. The National Park Service

Frederick, Maryland. The visitor center is located on Taneytown Road (State Route 134), just south of its junction with Emmitsburg Road (U.S. Business Route 15).

By Air: Harrisburg International Airport (717-948-3511) is served by several airlines.

By Train: Amtrak (800-872-7245) has stops in Baltimore, Maryland, and Harrisburg, Pennsylvania.

By Bus: Greyhound Lines (800-231-2222) has stops in Harrisburg. Bus tours, with

47

asks that visitors not climb on cannons and monuments and to use caution when travelling on park roads.

ACTIVITIES

Options include a driving tour, ranger-led walks and talks, hiking, bicycling, living-history and campfire programs, and licensed battlefield guides.

Hiking Trails

Three self-guided hiking trails, with interpretive trail pamphlets, are **High Water Mark Trail**, **Johnny Reb Trail**, and **Billy Yank Trail**. Other trails wind through the park as well.

OVERNIGHT STAYS

Lodging and Dining

While there are no lodging or dining facilities within the park, many accommodations, restaurants, privately run campgrounds, and

▲ *Meade's Headquarters at Gettysburg National Military Park, Pennsylvania*

other services are available in the town of Gettysburg and other nearby communities.

Campgrounds

Reservations for organized youth group camping, available from mid-April to mid-October, can be made by contacting the park.

NEARBY POINTS OF INTEREST

The area surrounding the park offers other worthwhile attractions that can be enjoyed as day trips or overnight excursions. Eisenhower National Historic Site is adjacent to the park's southwest boundary. Catoctin Mountain Park, Antietam National Battlefield, Hampton National Historic Site, and the Chesapeake & Ohio Canal National Historical Park are to the south in Maryland. Harpers Ferry National Historical Park is in West Virginia. Michaux State Forest, through which runs the Appalachian Trail, is a few miles to the west and north.

INDEPENDENCE NATIONAL HISTORICAL PARK

▲ *Statue of George Washington before Independence Hall*

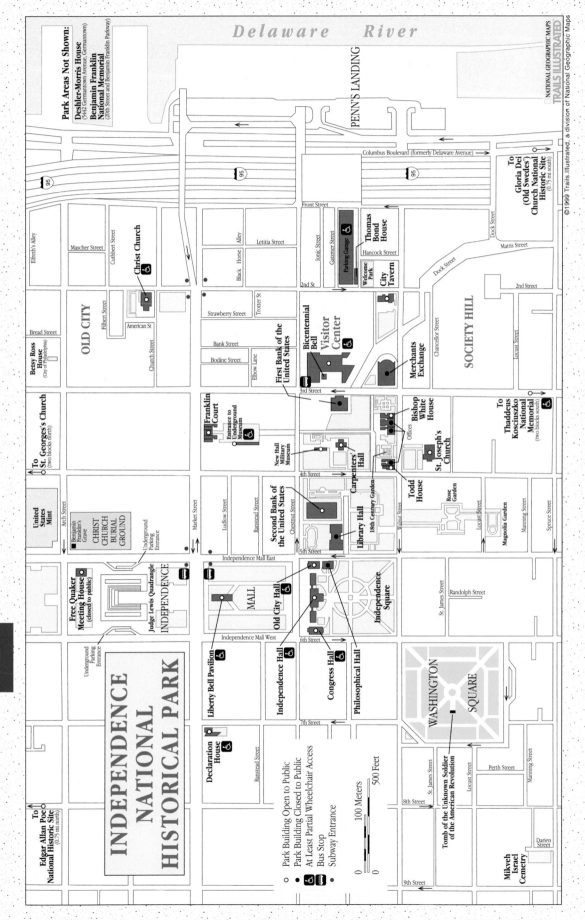

Delaware River

PENN'S LANDING

Park Areas Not Shown:
Deshler-Morris House
(5442 Germantown Avenue, Germantown)
Benjamin Franklin
National Memorial
(20th Street and Benjamin Franklin Parkway)

Columbus Boulevard (formerly Delaware Avenue)

To
Gloria Dei
(Old Swedes')
Church National
Historic Site
(0.75 mi south)

95

95

95

Front Street

Elfreth's Alley

Mascher Street

Cuthbert Street

Christ Church

OLD CITY

Filbert Street

American St

Bread Street

Betsy Ross
House
(City of Philadelphia)

Church Street

Letitia Street

Alley

Black Horse

Strawberry Street

Trotter St

Bank Street

Bodine Street

Elbow Lane

First Bank of the
United States

2nd St

Ionic Street

Gatzmer Street

Parking Garage

Thomas
Bond
House

Hancock Street

Welcome
Park

City
Tavern

Mattis Street

Dock Street

Dock Street

2nd Street

SOCIETY HILL

Chancellor Street

Locust Street

Bicentennial
Bell

Visitor
Center

Merchants
Exchange

3rd Street

To
St. George's Church
(two blocks north)

To St. George's Church

Franklin
Court

Entrance to
Underground
Museum

New Hall
Military Museum

Carpenters'
Hall

Bishop
White
House

Offices

St. Joseph's
Church

To
Thaddeus
Kosciuszko
National
Memorial
(two blocks south)

United
States
Mint

Arch Street

Benjamin Franklin's
Grave

CHRIST
CHURCH
BURIAL
GROUND

Underground
Parking
Entrance

Market Street

Ludlow Street

Ranstead Street

Chestnut Street

Second Bank of
the United States

Library Hall

18th Century Garden

Todd
House

Walnut Street

Rose
Garden

Locust Street

Magnolia Garden

Manning Street

Spruce Street

4th Street

5th Street

Independence Mall East

Underground
Parking
Entrance

Free Quaker
Meeting House
(closed to public)

Judge Lewis Quadrangle

INDEPENDENCE

MALL

Old City Hall

Independence
Square

St. James Street

Randolph Street

Liberty Bell Pavilion

Independence Hall

Congress Hall

Philosophical Hall

Independence Mall West

6th Street

INDEPENDENCE
NATIONAL
HISTORICAL PARK

To
Edgar Allan Poe
National Historic Site
(0.75 mi north)

Ranstead Street

Declaration
House

7th Street

WASHINGTON
SQUARE

Tomb of the Unknown Soldier
of the American Revolution

St. James Street

Perth Street

Locust Street

Manning Street

8th Street

9th Street

Mikveh
Israel
Cemetery

Darien
Street

Park Building Open to Public
Park Building Closed to Public
At Least Partial Wheelchair Access
Bus Stop
Subway Entrance

0   100 Meters
0   500 Feet

INDEPENDENCE NATIONAL HISTORICAL PARK

313 Walnut Street
Philadelphia, PA 19106-2778
215-597-8974

This 44-acre national historical park in downtown Philadelphia protects and interprets 26 properties associated with the American Revolution and the founding and early development of the United States. The National Park Service, in its interpretive handbook, *Independence*, calls this park "perhaps the most significant historical property in the United States—and also one of the most complex." In the same book, historian Carl Van Doren describes the area's significance: "In the last quarter of the 18th century, Philadelphia was the center of some of the most creative and far-reaching political thought of the modern world. Here, within the space of a few square blocks, in buildings still standing in their original splendor, Americans cast off ancient colonial ties, directed the course of a long and uncertain war to secure their liberties, and instituted a form of government adapted to the new needs of a rising people."

OUTSTANDING FEATURES

Among the many outstanding features of the park are the following: the **Liberty Bell** (on Market Street between 5th and 6th), a cherished symbol of American freedom; **Independence Hall** (on Chestnut Street between 5th and 6th), a World Heritage Site, where the Declaration of Independence was adopted in 1776, the Articles of Confederation were ratified in 1781, and the U.S. Constitution was framed in 1787; **Carpenter's Hall** (at 320 Chestnut), where delegates to the First Continental Congress met in 1774 to air their grievances against King George III; **Congress Hall** (next to Independence Hall), where the U.S. Congress convened while Philadelphia was the nation's

capital from 1790 to 1800; **Old City Hall** (next to Independence Hall), where the U.S. Supreme Court met from 1791 to 1800; **Franklin Court** (on Market Street between 3rd and 4th), site of Benjamin Franklin's home; and **Declaration House** (Market and 7th streets), a reconstruction of the house in which Thomas Jefferson drafted the Declaration of Independence.

ACTIVITIES

Options include self-guided and interpreter-led walking tours of 24 sites, interpretive exhibits, films, and special programs.

PRACTICAL INFORMATION

When to Go

Most park buildings are open 9 a.m.–5 p.m. daily. These hours, however, are subject to change without notice. During the summer, some buildings remain open into the evening. (The Philadelphia Exchange is not open to the public.)

How to Get There

By Car: From the east, take I-76/U.S Route 30 east on I-676/U.S. Route 30, turn right onto 6th Street, left onto Chestnut, and right onto 2nd. From the west, just after Benjamin Franklin Bridge (U.S. Route 30), follow signs to 6th Street-Historic Area, then go south on 6th, left onto Chestnut, and right onto 2nd. From the north, take Exit 17 from I-95 and continue straight on 2nd. From the south, take the Historic Area exit from I-95, follow signs to 6th Street-Historic Area, turn south on 6th, left onto Chestnut, and right onto 2nd.

By Air: Philadelphia International Airport (215-492-3181) is served by most major airlines.

By Train: Amtrak (800-872-7245) has stops in downtown Philadelphia.

By Bus: Greyhound Lines (800-231-2222) has stops in downtown Philadelphia.

Admission and Parking

Admission to Independence Hall, the Bishop White House, and the Todd House is by tour only. Tickets for the Bishop White House and the Todd House are issued at the visitor center on the day of your visit. No tickets are required for tours of Independence Hall and admission is on a first-come, first-served basis.

A parking garage is located on 2nd Street (one-way southbound), between Chestnut and Walnut streets. Street parking is also available throughout this part of Philadelphia.

Visitor Center

Independence Visitor Center, at Chestnut and 3rd streets; open daily. Information, interpretive exhibits, a half-hour audiovisual program, and publications.

Handicapped Accessibility

Most buildings are at least partly accessible, and captioned films are available on request. The visitor center has detailed accessibility guides.

Medical Services

First aid is available at each site. Five hospitals are within two miles of the park.

Pets

Pets are prohibited in all public buildings.

Lodging and Dining

There are numerous lodging and dining facilities in downtown Philadelphia.

Safety and Regulations

The National Park Service cautions visitors to watch their footing, especially on uneven surfaces and narrow stairways, and to be careful crossing busy city streets.

NEARBY POINTS OF INTEREST

The area surrounding the park offers other significant natural and cultural attractions that can be enjoyed as day trips or overnight excursions. Within the same city blocks are the Edgar Allan Poe National Historic Site, Thaddeus Kosciuszko National Memorial, and Gloria Dei (Old Swedes') Church National Historic Site. Valley Forge National Historical Park and Hopewell Furnace National Historic Site are located just a few miles west of Philadelphia, by way of the Pennsylvania Turnpike (I-76). Gettysburg National Military Park is farther west in southern Pennsylvania.

SHENANDOAH NATIONAL PARK

▲ Waterfall and mist

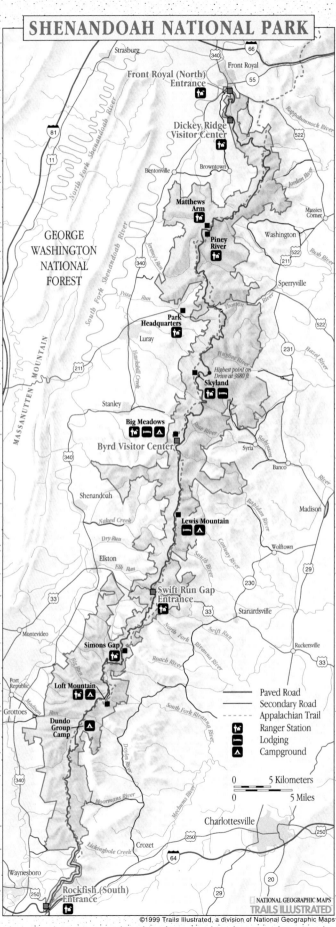

SHENANDOAH NATIONAL PARK

Strasburg

Front Royal (North)
Entrance

Dickey Ridge
Visitor Center

Browntown

Bentonville

GEORGE
WASHINGTON
NATIONAL
FOREST

Matthews
Arm

Piney
River

Washington

Sperryville

Park
Headquarters

Luray

Highest point on
Drive at 3680 ft

Skyland

Stanley

Big Meadows

Byrd Visitor Center

Syria

Banco

Shenandoah

Madison

Naked Creek

Lewis Mountain

Dry Run

Wolftown

Elkton

Elk Run

Swift Run Gap
Entrance

Stanardsville

Montevideo

Ruckersville

Simons Gap

Port
Republic

Loft Mountain

Grottoes

Dundo
Group
Camp

Charlottesville

Crozet

Waynesboro

Rockfish (South)
Entrance

MASSANUTTEN MOUNTAIN

North Fork Shenandoah River

South Fork Shenandoah River

Hawksbill Creek

Rappahannock River

Jordan River

Massies
Corner

Rush River

Thornton River

Hughey River

Robinson River

Hazel River

Rapidan River

Conway River

South River

Big Run

Madison Run

North Fork Rivanna River

Swift Run

Roach River

South Fork Rivanna River

Doyles River

Moormans River

Mechums River

Lickinghole Creek

Jeremys Run

Passage Run

Blue River

Paved Road
Secondary Road
Appalachian Trail
Ranger Station
Lodging
Campground

0   5 Kilometers

0   5 Miles

SHENANDOAH NATIONAL PARK

3655 U.S. Highway 211 East
Luray, VA 22835-9051
540-999-3500

This 197,389-acre national park encompasses a major part of the narrow Blue Ridge Mountains of northwest Virginia, protecting an ecologically rich area of dense, predominantly hardwood forests that cover rolling mountain-and-valley topography ranging from 530 feet to 4,050 feet above sea level. Innumerable deep valleys contain dashing streams with plunging waterfalls and cascades. Mountain slopes along the western side often drop abruptly to farmlands and villages in the Shenandoah Valley, while summits along the eastern side generally descend more gradually to lesser mountains and valleys that extend into the piedmont country. The park's 105-mile-long Skyline Drive, constructed from 1931 to 1939, affords approximately 75 spectacular panoramas and scenic overlooks. The park provides more than 500 miles of trails, 101 miles of which are the Appalachian Trail.

For more than a century, prior to establishment of the park in 1935, portions of these mountains and hollows had been logged, grazed, and farmed by mountain people who worked to make a living from the land. When the U.S. Congress authorized establishment of the park in 1926, it stipulated that no federal funds could be used to acquire lands for the park. Consequently, the Commonwealth of Virginia spent more than $2.25 million to acquire nearly 4,000 private properties. Some of the private owners gladly sold out, others left reluctantly. Thousands of Virginians helped by contributing the price of an acre of land, schoolchildren gave pennies, and a few individuals donated larger tracts of land. Subsequent extensive revegetation by the Civilian Conservation Corps (CCC) and natural healing and regeneration make it difficult now to believe that human occupation ever occurred.

Parts of the park were added to the National Wilderness Preservation System in 1976 and 1978.

OUTSTANDING FEATURES

Among the many outstanding features of the park are the following: **Skyline Drive**, the spectacular 105-mile north-south historic roadway, listed on the National Register, travels through the park that connects, at its southern terminus, with the 469-mile Blue Ridge Parkway; **Stony Man Mountain**, a 4,011-foot rocky summit just north of Skyland, the profile of which resembles that of a man as seen from Stony Man Overlook; **Skyland**, at 3,680 feet elevation, the highest part of Skyline Drive and the spot where lodging, a restaurant, and stables are located; **Whiteoak Canyon**, a cool, deeply shaded canyon just south of Skyland, with beautiful ancient hemlock trees and a spectacular series of six cascading waterfalls, the highest of which drops 86 feet; **Hawksbill Mountain**, at 4,051 feet elevation, the highest point in the park, best viewed from Crescent Rock Overlook between Skyland and Big Meadows; **Big Meadows**, an open grassy and shrubby expanse that is an unusual Shenandoah environment, located adjacent to the park's most developed area that includes the Harry F. Byrd Sr. Visitor Center; **Big Meadows Lodge**, which features a picnic area and a campground; **Dark Hollows Falls**, a 70-foot cascading waterfall once viewed by Thomas Jefferson, located near Big Meadows; and **Jones Run Falls**, a beautiful, 42-foot waterfall, plunging down sheer cliffs in the southern part of the park.

PRACTICAL INFORMATION

When to Go

The park is open year-round, with the majority of facilities available from late spring through late autumn. Winter snow and ice may cause stretches of roadways to be temporarily closed. October (usually the second and third weeks) is the most popular time to visit because of the magnificent display of colorful autumn foliage. The number of visitors at that time is at its peak, so it is a good idea to arrive early and

55

avoid weekends if possible. Summers are typically warm and humid. Wildflowers bloom from early spring to late fall.

How to Get There

By Car: From Washington, D.C., drive west on I-66 and south on U.S. Route 340 to the north entrance. From Charlottesville, drive west on I-64 to the south entrance. U.S. Route 211 passes over Thornton Gap between Luray and Sperryville. U.S. Route 33 passes over Swift Run Gap between Elton and Stanardsville.

By Air: Dulles International Airport (703-661-2700) and Charlottesville-Albemarle Airport (804-973-8341) are served by most major airlines.

By Train: Amtrak (800-872-7245) has stops in Charlottesville.

By Bus: Greyhound Lines (800-231-2222) has stops in Charlottesville.

Fees and Permits

Entrance fees are $10 per vehicle and $5 per person on foot, bicycle, motorcycle, or by bus. A Virginia state license is required for fishing and is available at most wayside facilities in the park.

A free backcountry-use permit is required, available by mail or in person at entrance stations, visitor centers, and park headquarters.

Visitor Centers

Dickey Ridge Visitor Center: open spring through late fall. Interpretive exhibits, audiovisual programs, and publications.

Harry F. Byrd Sr. Visitor Center: open April through early November. Interpretive exhibits, audiovisual programs, and publications.

Facilities

Included are horse stables, firewood sales, grocery and camp stores, gift shops, service stations, hot showers, laundry, and ice sales. Most places are open spring through late fall.

Handicapped Accessibility

Visitor centers, picnic areas, amphitheaters, parking, most restrooms, some campsites and restrooms at all campgrounds, lodges, and a self-guided nature trail at Big Meadows and the Limberlost Trail are fully or partly wheelchair-accessible. Part of the nature trail at Big Meadows is a paved surface, and the Limberlost Trail is a hard-packed greenstone surface. Contact the park for a detailed brochure.

Medical Services

First aid is available in the park. Hospitals are in Front Royal, Luray, and Harrisonburg.

Pets

Pets are allowed, but must be kept leashed and under control at all times. They are not allowed in public buildings on a few trails.

Safety and Regulations

For your safety and enjoyment and for the protection of the park, please follow these regulations and suggestions:

- Fires are permitted only in established fireplaces or grills and are prohibited in the backcountry. Be sure to extinguish all smoking materials completely.

- Remember that feeding, disturbing, capturing, or hunting wildlife is prohibited.

- Bicycles and motor vehicles must stay on paved roads. Use caution when driving in fog, which may occur at any time.

- Respect the rights of landowners when near park boundaries.

- Watch your footing and wear proper footwear.

- Only one type of wood is acceptable for building a minimum impact campfire—dead and downed wood that can be broken by hand. Walk out-of-sight from trails and campsites to gather firewood, and collect only loose sticks and branches from the ground in areas where they are plentiful. Breaking live or dead tree limbs can make trees more susceptible to insects and disease and create barren under-stories that are unnatural in appearance. Fires should be kept small and under careful control. Bonfires waste precious firewood and create long-lasting damage to fragile soil organisms.

Options include hiking, birdwatching, horse-back riding, bicycling, picnicking, camping, interpretive programs, cross-country skiing, and fishing. Further information is available in the park's newspaper, *Overlook*.

Hiking Trails

Skyline Drive mileages are from the northern (Front Royal) park entrance, southward. Among the many trails are the following:

In the park's North District: **Fox Hollow Nature Trail** (Mile 4.6), an easy 1.3-mile, self-guided interpretive loop, beginning across the drive from the Dickey Ridge Visitor Center and providing views of the old Fox family homesites; **Compton Peak Trail** (Mile 10.4), a mostly moderately easy but briefly rough, rocky, and steep 1.2-mile route climbing more than 800 feet; trail begins on the Appalachian Trail on the west side of the drive (opposite the parking area), soon branches onto Compton Peak Trail, and affords views of boulders and columnar-jointed rock formations; **Traces Nature Trail** (Mile 22.2), an easy 1.7-mile loop beginning at Mathews Arm Campground amphitheater and offering views of the traces of an old homesite once occupied by mountain people; **Overall Run Falls Trail** (Mile 22.2), a mostly easy, but briefly steep, 1.9-mile, 1,140-foot route beginning at Mathews Arm campground, then following the old Mathews Arm Fire Road/Trail for 1.4 miles and left onto the Overall Run Trail, and finally descending steeply a half-mile to this 93-foot cascading waterfall, the highest drop of any in the park. As with other waterfalls and cascades in Shenandoah, Overall Run Falls is at its most spectacular after periods of rainfall, as in the spring, and may be virtually or completely dry after arid spells.

In the park's Central District: **Stony Man Nature Trail** (Mile 41.7), an easy .8-mile, 340-foot climb beginning at the parking area just off the northern entrance road to Skyland Lodge, reaching the cliffs of 4,011-foot Stony Man Mountain where the trail is a bit rough, and affording grand panoramas from the sec-

ond highest point in the park; **Whiteoak Canyon Trail** (Mile 42.6), a fairly easy, 2.3-mile, 1,040-foot descent beginning at the Whiteoak Canyon parking area on Skyline Drive and leading to one of Shenandoah's most beautiful places, where there are deeply shaded groves of ancient hemlock trees and the park's second highest waterfall, cascading 86 feet down the cliffs; below this waterfall, the trail becomes rough and steep as it descends 1.3 miles and 1,100 feet through a narrower stretch of canyon and passes five more waterfalls ranging in height from 35 to 62 feet; **Hawksbill Summit Trails** (Mile 45.6), a steep, .9-mile, 690-foot, rocky and rough climb beginning at the parking area on Skyline Drive and providing wide panoramas from the 4,051-foot summit—the park's highest; from Upper Hawksbill parking area (Mile 46.7), an easier, one-mile, trail-and-fire-road route leads 520 feet up to the summit; **Dark Hollow Falls Trail** (Mile 50.7), a moderately easy, .7-mile, 440-foot descent beginning at Dark Hollow Falls parking area on Skyline Drive following the stream course of Hogcamp Branch, and winding to the base of this 70-foot, splashing cascade, which is at its best following periods of rainfall but may not even have a trickle of water during dry periods; below this falls, the trail descends another several hundred yards, passing additional small cascades and waterfalls before reaching the Rose River fire road; **Story-of-the-Forest Nature Trail** (Mile 51), an easy 1.8-mile, self-guided interpretive loop (formerly known as Big Meadows Swamp Trail), beginning just east of the Harry F. Byrd Sr. Visitor Center and offering opportunities to see numerous species of wildflowers and other plantlife in this unusual high-elevation swamp; **Lewis Falls Trail** (Mile 51.4), a fairly easy-to-moderate, 3.3-mile loop beginning and ending at the Big Meadows Campground amphitheater parking area, winding along the slopes below Blackrock, affording views of this 81-foot falls (the fourth highest cascading waterfall in the park), and climbing through a deeply shaded grove of old hemlocks; **South River Falls Trail** (Mile 62.8), a moderately easy, 1.3-mile route beginning at the east end of the South River Picnic Area and descending about 850 feet through a variety of forest habitats to the

▲ *Storm lifting at Shenandoah National Park, Virginia*

park's third highest waterfall; this impressive waterfall plunges into a pool at the base of the first stage of its 83-foot drop and then divides into two separate cascades before plunging into a deep gorge; as with other park waterfalls, South River Falls is best seen during high water following periods of rainfall; **Old Rag Summit Trail**, a 3,268-foot granite summit rising to the east of the crest of the Blue Ridge that is reached by two trails that climb from the park's eastern boundary; the easier of the two is the 2.7-mile Saddle Trail route from the head of Berry Hollow at the end of 4.7-mile State Route 600 (reached south from Sperryville on State Routes 231 and 643), climbing 1,760 feet from the parking area, .9-mile north on the old Berry Hollow Road to its junction with Old Rag Fire Road and east 1.8 miles on the rocky and often steep Saddle Trail to the summit of Old Rag, from which tremendous views are available.

In the park's South District: **Hightop Summit Trail** (Mile 66.7), a moderate, 1.5-

mile, 935-foot climb to this 3,587-foot summit, beginning at a parking area on Skyline Drive and following the Appalachian Trail most of the way, offering views of many peaks from a rocky outcrop; **Deadening Trail** (Mile 79.5), a fairly easy, 1.4-mile, self-guided interpretive loop beginning at Skyline Drive just north of the Loft Mountain Campground, passing through a variety of habitats from pasture to old-growth forest, and briefly following the Appalachian Trail on Loft Mountain; **Blackrock Summit Trail** (Mile 84.8), an easy one-mile route beginning on an old fire road at the parking area just off Skyline Drive, then following the Appalachian Trail across an expanse of rocky talus slope and swinging around three sides of Blacktop; while there is no separate trail to this 3,092-foot summit, hikers can leave the main trail at any point and scramble over the rocks for a grand panorama; and **Turk Mountain Trail** (Mile 94.1), a fairly easy, 1.1-mile, 690-foot climb beginning at Turk Gap parking area on Skyline Drive, descending into a saddle, and climbing to this 2,960-foot summit, the rocky talus slopes of which afford excellent panoramas.

Lodging and Dining

For reservations (taken beginning June 1) and information on the following lodging facilities, contact ARAMARK, Inc., Box 727, Luray, VA 22835; 540-743-5108 or 800-999-4714:

Skyland: offering rooms, cabins, and suites from early April through November. Dining room, bar lounge with live entertainment, conference hall, gift shop, guided horseback trips, and children's pony rides.

Big Meadows Lodge: offering motel rooms and cabins from late April through October. Dining room, bar lounge with live entertainment, and gift shop.

Lewis Mountain Cottages: offering cabins with indoor/outdoor areas from early May through October. Campstore, laundry, showers, firewood, and ice.

The Potomac Appalachian Trail Club operates six cabins (reservations with the trail club are needed) and maintains huts for Appalachian Trail hikers, and publishes maps and other park materials. Contact the club at 118 Park Street, SE, Vienna, VA 22180-4609; 703-242-0315.

Panorama Restaurant offers meals from early spring through early November.

Big Meadows Wayside Restaurant offers meals from late March through November.

Loft Mountain Wayside and Elkwallow Wayside both have grill service and serve meals from early spring through October.

Campgrounds

Matthews Arm and Loft Mountain campgrounds are on a first-come, first-served basis. Reservations for Big Meadows campground can be made by contacting the National Park Reservation Service at 800-365-CAMP. Campgrounds are often full on summer weekends and early autumn weekends.

Backcountry Camping

Backcountry camping is allowed year-round throughout much of the park, with a free back-country permit. There is no limit on the total length of stay in the backcountry; the two-day limit is for any one campsite. Campers are reminded to keep a clean camp, to hang food high in a tree to avoid attracting black bears, and to follow all Leave No Trace principles.

FLORA AND FAUNA (Partial Listings)

Mammals: black bear, whitetail deer, bobcat, gray foxes, longtail weasel, raccoon, opossum, spotted and striped skunks, woodchuck, eastern cottontail, squirrels (gray, fox, flying, and red), and eastern chipmunk.

Birds: American woodcock, wild turkey, ruffed grouse, bobwhite, hawks (red-tailed, red-shouldered, and broad-winged), turkey and black vultures, barred owl, mourning dove, yellow-billed and black-billed cuckoos, ruby-throated hummingbird, woodpeckers (pileated, red-bellied, downy, and hairy), flicker, yellow-bellied sapsucker, eastern kingbird, eastern phoebe, eastern wood pewee, great crested and Acadian flycatchers, barn and tree swallows, crow, raven, blue jay, Carolina chickadee, tufted titmouse, white-breasted and red-breasted nuthatches, brown creeper, house and Carolina wrens, ruby-crowned and golden-crowned kinglets, brown thrasher, catbird, mockingbird, eastern bluebird, robin, wood thrush, veery, cedar waxwing, solitary and red-eyed vireos, warblers (northern parula, black-throated green, black-and-white, yellow-rumped, chestnut-sided, blackburnian, pine, prairie, yellow, and hooded), American redstart, common yellowthroat, ovenbird, Louisiana waterthrush, yellow-breasted chat, scarlet tanager, dark-eyed junco, cardinal, purple finch, American goldfinch, indigo bunting, rose-breasted grosbeak, rufous-sided towhee, and white-throated, chipping, field, and song sparrows.

Amphibians and Reptiles: turtles (eastern box, painted, and snapping), spring peeper, frogs (northern cricket, gray tree, green, pickerel, upland chorus, and wood), bullfrog, American toad, northern coal and five-lined skinks, salamanders (Jefferson, northern red, spotted, northern dusky, northern two-lined, Shenandoah, northern long-tailed, northern spring, four-toed, slimy, and red-backed), northern fence lizard, northern black racer, snakes (eastern garter, eastern ribbon, northern ringneck, smooth earth, northern redbelly, smooth and rough green, corn, eastern milk, eastern king, queen, eastern worm, and northern water), copperhead, and timber rattlesnake.

Trees, Shrubs, Flowers, and Ferns:

pines (eastern white, table mountain, Virginia, pitch, and shortleaf), red spruce, eastern hemlock, Fraser fir, eastern redcedar, Canada yew, tulip tree (yellow poplar), sassafras, American sycamore, witch hazel, black walnut, pignut hickory, American chestnut (sprouts), oaks (white, chestnut, northern red, southern red, and scarlet), eastern hop hornbeam, birches (yellow, gray, and black), American basswood, common chokecherry, black cherry, American mountain-ash, serviceberry, spicebush, eastern redbud, black locust, flowering dogwood, black tupelo, maples (mountain, striped, red, and sugar), white ash, common alder, mountain holly, mountain laurel, pink and rose azaleas, catawba rhododendron (at southern end of the park), shadbush, red osier dogwood, blackberry, thimbleberry, staghorn sumac, huckleberry, blueberry, bunchberry, bearberry, Virginia creeper, jack-in-the-pulpit, Mayapple, Solomon's, Canada mayflower, hepatica, trilliums (red, painted, and white), showy orchis, yellow and pink lady's slippers, ladies'-tresses, bloodroot, trailing arbutus, wintergreen, pipsissewa, violets, wood and turk's-cap lilies, closed gentian, harebell, blazingstar, cardinal flower, columbine, black snakeroot, whorled loosestrife, viper's bugloss, wild ginger, Allegheny stonecrop, moss phlox, three-toothed cinquefoil, blue-eyed grass, black-eyed Susan, ox-eye daisy, chickory, Virginia spiderwort, evening primrose, Queen Anne's lace, goldenrods, sunflowers, asters, Joe-Pye-weed, Indian pipe, and bracken, interrupted, wood, lady, hayscented, Christmas, common polypody, maidenhair spleenwort, and rusty woodsia.

NEARBY POINTS OF INTEREST

The area surrounding the park offers many fascinating natural and historical attractions that can be enjoyed as day trips or overnight excursions. George Washington National Forest is to the west and southwest of the park, and Manassas National Battlefield Park and Fredericksburg and Spotsylvania County Battlefields Memorial National Military Park are to the east. A number of important Civil War battlefield sites in the Shenandoah Valley are under consideration for National Park Service protection.

OTHER NATIONAL PARK UNITS IN THE NORTHEAST REGION

▲ The Great Falls Tavern at the Chesapeake and Ohio Canal National Historical Park, Maryland

Other National Park Units in the Northeast Region

Weir Farm National Historic Site

735 Nod Hill Road
Wilton, CT 06897-1309
203-834-1896

This 60-acre national historic site in southwest Connecticut protects and interprets the summer home and workplace of American Impressionist painter J. Alden Weir (1852–1919). The peaceful landscape of this farm became one of Weir's main sources of artistic inspiration for nearly 40 years, and it has continued to provide inspiration to artists ever since. This is the first national historic site dedicated to the legacy of an American artist.

The farm's wooded acres contain numerous hiking trails, including the self-guided Weir Farm Historic Painting Sites trail, and tours of the artist's studio are available. A visitor center with exhibits and an orientation video is located in Burlington House, an old farm house on the property that was formerly occupied by one of Weir's daughters. The Weir Farm Heritage Trust, a nonprofit organization that works in partnership with the National Park Service, offers lectures, art classes, workshops, a program for visiting artists, and special exhibits. Access to the site from I-95 or the Merritt Parkway is by way of their exits onto U.S. Route 7 northbound or from I-84 by way of Exit 3 or U.S. Route 7 southbound; then proceeding to State Route 102 West to Old Branchville Road and to Nod Hill Road and the site's entrance.

Constitution Gardens

Mailing address:
c/o National Capital Parks-Central
900 Ohio Drive, S.W.
Washington, DC 20242-0004
202-426-6841

This 52-acre park, located between the Washington Monument and Lincoln Memorial is dedicated to the 56 signers of the Declaration of Independence. The site's 6.5-acre lake surrounds a one-acre island on which is the Signers' Memorial. On each of the memorial's 56 low granite stones, arranged in a half-circle around a plaza, is inscribed a signer's signature, the name of his home, and his profession. By presidential proclamation, the gardens are also "a Living Legacy dedicated to the commemoration of the United States Constitution." In the words of the National Park Service: "As a Living Legacy, Constitution Gardens has become a tribute to the successful experiment in government begun by the Founders; it is a quiet, contemplative spot, in the midst of the bustling capital."

Ford's Theatre National Historic Site

Mailing address:
c/o National Capital Parks-Central
900 Ohio Drive, S.W.
Washington, DC 20242-0004
202-426-6924

This national historic site protects Ford's Theatre, at 511 Tenth Street, S.W., in Washington, D.C., where President Abraham Lincoln was shot by an assassin on April 14, 1865, and the William Peterson house across the street where he died the following morning. The assassin, John Wilkes Booth, was a Confederate sympathizer who favored slavery. Lincoln died just six days after Confederate Gen. Robert E. Lee surrendered to U.S. Gen. Ulysses S. Grant at Appomattox Court House in Virginia—thus finally ending the Civil War and bringing about the "just and lasting peace" that President Lincoln had so fervently worked for.

Open daily except Christmas, Ford's Theatre is not only a museum, with 15-minute interpretive talks and exhibits in the building's basement, but it continues to operate as an active theater. Throughout the year, the Ford's Theatre Society presents a wide variety of contemporary plays reflecting America's ethnic and cultural diversity. The theater is not open to national historic site visitors when the stage is being prepared for a play or during rehearsals or matinee performances. For information on plays and tickets, call the box office at 202-347-4833.

Franklin Delano Roosevelt Memorial

Mailing address:
National Capital Parks-Central
900 Ohio Drive, S.W.
Washington, DC 20242-0004
202-426-6841

This 7.5-acre memorial adjacent to the Tidal Basin in West Potomac Park honors the memory and accomplishments of Franklin D. Roosevelt, who served as the 32nd president of the United States from 1933 to 1945. The memorial consists of four outdoor galleries that portray FDR's four terms in office. Granite walls, inscriptions, bronze sculptures, waterfalls, and ornamental landscaping combine to offer visitors a feeling of being in a secluded garden. Among the inscriptions are Roosevelt's words on the environment: "Men and nature must work hand in hand. The throwing out of balance of the resources of nature throws out of balance also the lives of man." Also notable at the site is a statue of Eleanor Roosevelt, the only First Lady so honored at a presidential memorial. Access to the site is by way of Independence Avenue, between the Washington Monument and the Lincoln Memorial, following signs to the west bank of the Tidal Basin. The Tourmobile also provides transportation.

Frederick Douglass National Historic Site

1411 W Street, S.E.
Washington, DC 20020-4813
202-426-5961

This eight-acre national historic site protects and interprets "Cedar Hill," the 1850s brick house that was the home of Frederick Douglass from 1877 to 1895 and honors Douglass's legacy and accomplishments. This acclaimed, self-educated orator, author, and champion of the oppressed escaped from slavery at the age of 20 and became an abolitionist, owner-editor of an antislavery newspaper, women's rights activist, fluent speaker of many languages, U.S. Marshal of the District of Columbia, and U.S. minister to Haiti.

The visitor center provides interpretive exhibits, an audiovisual program, and publications on Douglass and African-American culture. Visitors can tour the house, which is open daily except Thanksgiving, Christmas, and New Year's Day. Access is from I-495 (Capital Beltway) by way of Exit 3, north onto Indian Head Highway (State Route 210), which becomes South Capitol Street, and right onto W Street to the parking area.

Korean War Veterans Memorial

Mailing address:
c/o National Capital Parks-Central
900 Ohio Drive, S.W.
Washington, DC 20242-0004
202-426-6841

This two-acre memorial located near the Lincoln Memorial is a tribute to the Americans who served in the Korean War (1950 to 1953). More than 56,000 U.S. military personnel lost their lives in the conflict, while more than 100,000 were wounded. The memorial consists of 19 seven-foot-tall stainless steel sculptures of battle-clad foot soldiers "walking" across the field of service toward a flagpole from which waves an American flag. A polished black-granite wall depicts photographic images of 2,500 soldiers. A grove of linden trees frames the circular Pool of Remembrance. The memorial is staffed by park rangers daily, except Christmas. Interpretive publications are available at the bookstore on the chamber level of the Lincoln Memorial nearby.

Lincoln Memorial

Mailing address:
c/o National Capital Parks-Central
900 Ohio Drive, S.W.
Washington, DC 20242-0004
202-426-6841

This 107-acre memorial overlooking the Potomac River near the east end of the Arlington

Memorial Bridge commemorates the life and accomplishments of Abraham Lincoln, who served as the 16th president of the United States from 1861 to l865. The memorial, designed by architect Henry Bacon, resembles the ancient Parthenon on the Acropolis in Athens, Greece. Its focal point is the magnificent, 19-foot-high, seated, white-marble statue of Lincoln designed by sculptor Daniel Chester French. The troubled facial expression of the statue is meant to reflect the enormous burden of worries and heartbreak the president felt during the country's greatest trial, the Civil War.

The sheltering memorial is embellished with 36 Doric columns that represent the 36 states of the United States at the time of Lincoln's death. The eloquent words of the president's Gettysburg Address and his Second Inaugural Address are carved into the interior marble walls. National Park Service interpreters are on duty daily, except Christmas. An exhibit, "Lincoln's Legacy," is presented on the ground floor level, and a bookstore is on the chamber level. National Park Service permits are required for holding First Amendment and other special functions. Access to the memorial is by way of Constitution Avenue and 23rd Street, N.W.; and from Virginia, across the Potomac River on the Arlington Memorial Bridge. The Tourmobile provides transportation as well.

Lyndon Baines Johnson Memorial Grove on the Potomac

Mailing address:
c/o George Washington Memorial Parkway
Turkey Run Park
McLean, VA 22101-0001
703-285-2598

This 17-acre living memorial to Lyndon B. Johnson, 36th president of the United States, is located on Columbia Island in the Potomac River near the Virginia shore. Providing a vista of the nation's capital, the memorial features some of President Johnson's words inscribed into a large block of Texas granite and a beautiful grove of white pines and dogwoods. Paths wind through the grove, where beautiful flowering shrubs such as rhododendrons and azaleas are planted, along with flowers—notably

daffodils that bloom by the thousands in springtime. A picnic area is available. The memorial grove is adjacent to the George Washington Memorial Parkway, just upriver from George Mason Bridge (14th Street Bridge of I-395, westbound). Parking is available at the Columbia Island Marina.

Mary McLeod Bethune Council House National Historic Site

1318 Vermont Avenue, N.W.
Washington, DC 20005-3607
202-673-2402

This national historic site commemorates the life and accomplishments of Mary McLeod Bethune (1875–1955), an African-American woman who rose from humble beginnings to become a distinguished educator, political activist, and advisor to four presidents of the United States. The site protects and interprets the three-story Victorian-style townhouse that she purchased to serve as the first headquarters of the National Council of Negro Women from 1943 to 1966. The house also contains the National Archives for Black Women's History. In 1904, Bethune was a founder of the Daytona Educational and Industrial School for Negro Girls (subsequently Bethune-Cookman College) in Daytona Beach, Florida. The site provides interpretive exhibits, audiovisual programs, and publications. Lectures, workshops, and guided tours for groups of ten or more are offered. The archives are available for reference use by appointment. The site is open daily, except on federal holidays. Access to the site is just south of Logan Circle, on Vermont Avenue.

National Capital Parks

National Capital Area
1100 Ohio Drive, S.W.
Washington, DC 20242-0001
202-619-7222

The National Capital Parks system of more than 300 parks, sites, and parkways totaling 6,546 acres in the District of Columbia includes the Battleground National Cemetery, the President's Park, Lafayette Park, north of the White House and the Ellipse, a number of historic fortifications, and parkland. Some of these sites are described separately in this guidebook, while numerous others are not.

National Mall

Mailing address:
c/o National Capital Parks-Central
900 Ohio Drive, S.W.
Washington, DC 20242-0004
202-426-6841

This 146-acre, landscaped mall, extending from the National Capitol to the Washington Monument was first envisioned as a formal park in 1790 by French engineer Pierre L'Enfant as part of his grand plan for the city of Washington. Most of the major museums and galleries of the Smithsonian Institution front on its grassy expanse that is bordered by elm trees. The National Mall is a popular public gathering place for festivals, concerts, and many other recreational activities. National Park Service permits are required for holding First Amendment and other special events there. Access to the mall is by way of either Constitution or Independence avenues, between 3rd and 14th streets.

Pennsylvania Avenue National Historic Site

Mailing address:
c/o National Capital Parks-Central
900 Ohio Drive, S.W.
Washington, DC 20242-0004
202-426-6841

This 20-acre national historic site between The White House and the National Capitol includes the portion of Pennsylvania Avenue between 1st and 15th streets, N.W., and its vicinity. Within this area are Ford's Theatre National Historic Site, several blocks of the Washington commercial district, the Federal Bureau of Investigation (FBI), and a number of buildings in the Federal Triangle, including the National Archives and the Old Post Office Tower. Scheduled tours of the site are offered by Architour, a nonprofit organization; for information, call 202-265-6454.

Rock Creek Park

3545 Williamsburg Lane, N.W.
Washington, DC 20008-1207
202-282-1063

This 1,754-acre heavily wooded park, running through the northwestern part of Washington, D.C., from the District-Maryland line to the Potomac River, is one of the largest urban parks in the United States. It contains a wide range of natural, historical, and recreational features, including Civil War forts and restored Pierce Mill, where water power is still used to grind corn and wheat. Soon after the Civil War, the idea of this park emerged from a search for a new location for the President's House, an effort assigned by the secretary of war to Major Nathaniel Michel. The plan to move the President's House to a new site was never acted upon, but Michel considered it remarkable that an area of such extraordinary natural beauty lay so close to the offices of the national government and proposed that the valley of Rock Creek be set aside as a public park. Two decades elapsed before Congress finally approved establishment of this "wilderness" park within the nation's capital.

Rock Creek valley is covered with deciduous trees, with such species as tulip tree (yellow-poplar), beech, red maple, sassafras, flowering dogwood, eastern redbud, American sycamore, and a number of oaks, including southern and northern red, black, scarlet, chestnut, willow, and white. Among the many spring wildflowers are Mayapple, Jack-in-the-pulpit, bluet, spring beauty, bloodroot, trailing arbutus, Dutchman's-breeches, round-lobed hepatica, showy orchis, and whorled pogonia.

Mammals include red and gray foxes, raccoon, eastern gray and flying squirrels, opossum, and eastern cottontail. Among the extensive list of birds are red-tailed hawk, turkey vulture, barred owl, mourning dove, ruby-throated hummingbird, belted kingfisher, woodpeckers (pileated, red-bellied, and downy), flicker, eastern phoebe, eastern wood pewee, barn swallow, chimney swift, crow, blue jay, Carolina chickadee, tufted titmouse, white-breasted nuthatch, Carolina wren, brown thrasher, catbird, mockingbird, robin, wood thrush, red-eyed vireo, warblers (prothonotary, black-and-white, yellow-rumped, prairie, yellow, hooded, and Kentucky), American redstart, common yellowthroat, yellow-breasted chat, Louisiana waterthrush, ovenbird, Baltimore oriole, scarlet tanager, cardinal, American goldfinch, indigo bunting, rose-breasted grosbeak, rufous-sided towhee, and white-throated, chipping, and song sparrows.

Hiking trails and bridle paths wind through the valley, and a signed bicycle route runs the length of the park. The park's main information center, Rock Creek Nature Center (202-426-6829), provides interpretive exhibits, programs, publications, and a natural history library and offers guided nature walks and hikes. The center is open daily from Memorial Day to Labor Day; the rest of the year, the center is closed on Mondays, Tuesdays, and holidays. The Art Barn (202-244-2482) near Pierce Mill is a historic carriage house that displays the works of local artists and is operated by the Art Barn Association in cooperation with the National Park Service. Other historic places include Fort DeRussy and Fort Bayard, two among the ring of fortifications encircling Washington to help defend the Union capital during the Civil War.

An 18-hole golf course (202-882-7332), playing fields (202-767-8363), and tennis courts (202-722-5949) are also available, and horse rentals and riding lessons are provided at the Rock Creek Park Horse Center (202-362-0117). Numerous picnic areas are scattered throughout the park. Access is by a number of streets, including Military Road, just south of which is the nature center, horse center, and planetarium, all located along Glover Road. Public transportation to the nature center is by way of the Friendship Heights Metro stop, transferring to the E2 bus, to Military and Glover roads. Tilden Street branches from Connecticut Avenue and Piney Branch Road from 16th Street—both of which lead down to Pierce Mill and the Art Barn.

Theodore Roosevelt Island

c/o George Washington Memorial Parkway
Turkey Run Park
McLean, VA 22101-0001
703-285-2598

This densely forested 88-acre island in the Potomac River near the Virginia shore is dedicated to the memory of Theodore Roosevelt, the 26th president of the United States, who did so much to advance natural resource conservation and park protection in America during his years in the White House from 1901 to 1909. Near the northern end of the island, the Theodore Roosevelt Memorial consists of a 17-foot-tall bronze statue rising from a fountain-embellished terrace and four granite panels containing excerpts from Roosevelt's writings on conservation, youth, manhood, and government. One selection reads: "The Nation behaves well if it treats the natural resources as assets which it must turn over to the next generation increased and not impaired in value."

Among the island's river-bottomland deciduous trees are American sycamore, tulip tree (yellow-poplar), sassafras, sweetgum, several varieties of oaks, river birch, eastern redbud, black tupelo, and red maple. Mammals include red and gray foxes, muskrat, opossum, raccoon, eastern cottontail, and eastern gray and flying squirrels. Of the many birds, there are black-crowned night-heron, great blue and green-backed herons, wood duck and other waterfowl, bald eagle, osprey, barred owl, belted kingfisher, pileated and red-bellied woodpeckers, blue jay, Carolina chickadee, tufted titmouse, white-breasted nuthatch, Carolina wren, wood thrush, red-eyed vireo, warblers (prothonotary, black-and-white, yellow-rumped, yellow, and hooded), American redstart, common yellowthroat, Louisiana waterthrush, ovenbird, red-winged blackbird, Baltimore oriole, scarlet tanager, cardinal, American goldfinch, rose-breasted grosbeak, rufous-sided towhee, and white-throated, swamp, and song sparrows.

The island is open daily. The National Park Service offers guided tours, and trails wind through the forest. Access is by way of a footbridge from the Virginia shore, reached from a parking area just off the northbound lanes of the George Washington Memorial Parkway. Another way to reach the island is by canoe. A canoe rental business is located just upriver, beneath the Washington end of the Francis Scott Key Bridge.

Thomas Jefferson Memorial

Mailing address:
c/o National Capital Parks-Central
900 Ohio Drive, S.W.
Washington, DC 20242-0004
202-426-6841

This impressive, circular, low-domed memorial, surrounded by a colonnade of classical Ionic columns and fronting on the Tidal Basin honors the memory and accomplishments of Thomas Jefferson, author of the Declaration of Independence and third president of the United States. A 19-foot-tall bronze statue of Jefferson stands in the center of the memorial's rotunda. On the encircling inner walls are excerpts from his writings, including the Declaration of Independence and the Virginia Statute for Religious Freedom. The memorial and its landscaped setting encompass 18 acres.

National Park Service interpretive talks on Jefferson and the memorial are presented daily, except Christmas. In late March and early April, one of the city's most beautiful scenes occurs when the pink-flowered Japanese cherry trees burst into bloom around the Tidal Basin framing the memorial. Access is by way of Independence Avenue (between the Washington Monument and the Lincoln Memorial) and following the signs. The Tourmobile provides transportation services as well.

Vietnam Veterans Memorial

Mailing address:
c/o National Capital Parks-Central
900 Ohio Drive, S.W.
Washington, DC 20242-0004
202-426-6841

This two-acre memorial at the western end of Constitution Gardens and just northeast of the Lincoln Memorial honors all the men and women of the U.S. Armed Services who served in the Vietnam War from 1963 to 1973. The Vietnam Veterans Memorial consists of two 246.75-foot-long, polished black-granite walls, extending outward like enveloping triangular wings, from a 125-degree angle at the vertex. The walls are inscribed with 58,132 names of persons who died or remain missing. The mirrored surface of the granite reflects the surrounding trees and monuments, visitors standing before the monument, and myriad gifts and mementos that visitors leave along its base to honor the dead.

The site also features a life-size bronze sculpture of three American soldiers in Vietnam and a statue honoring the women who served in the war. The memorial was privately funded by 275,000 contributions from individuals, corporations, foundations, veterans groups, and other organizations, to the Vietnam Veterans Memorial Fund, Inc. National Park Service rangers, stationed at a nearby kiosk, provide directions and computer printouts with information such as a soldier's date of birth, date of casualty, and branch of military service. Located adjacent to Constitution Avenue and 23rd Street, N.W., the memorial is open daily. The Tourmobile provides transportation service.

Washington Monument

Mailing address:
c/o National Capital Parks-Central
900 Ohio Drive, S.W.
Washington, DC 20242-0004
202-426-6841

This majestic, 555-foot-tall marble obelisk, rises far above everything else in downtown Washington, D.C., and reminds us of George Washington's immense contribution to the United States of America. He was the successful commander-in-chief of American forces in the Revolutionary War (1775 to 1781), the presiding officer of the Constitutional Convention (1787), and the first U.S. president (1789 to 1797). Washington defined the presidency during his two terms, helped develop the relationships among the federal government's executive, legislative, and judicial branches, and established precedents that successfully launched the new government on its course. In 1848, Congress authorized construction of the monument, and by 1854, it had reached 150 feet tall. But there it remained for a quarter of a century, construction first halted by a controversy over the theft of a commemorative stone from the Roman Catholic Church and further delayed by the Civil War. Finally completed in 1884, the monument and its setting encompass 106 acres.

In 1998, major repair work was performed on the structure. Once that work is completed, visitors will once again be able to take the elevator to the 500-foot level, where two windows in each of four directions provide awesome views of the city. A ticket system to enter the monument operates from early April to Labor Day. Free tickets for timed entry are available at the Ticketmaster booth located east of the monument on 15th Street; for advance tickets for a fee, call 800-505-5040. The monument is bounded by Constitution and Independence avenues and 15th and 17th streets. The Tourmobile also provides transportation service.

The White House

Mailing address:
c/o National Capital Area
1100 Ohio Drive, S.W.
Washington, DC 20242-0001
202-755-7798

The White House, located at 1600 Pennsylvania Avenue, N.W., between Lafayette Square and the Washington Monument, is the oldest public building in the nation's capital and the most famous address in the United States. For more than 200 years, this Irish Georgian-style country mansion, originally called the President's House, has been the focus of the U.S. presidency and the home of all presidents, after George Washington. Construction began in 1793, and President John Adams moved into the still unfinished structure in 1800.

On the evening of August 24, 1814, British troops invaded the city and set fire to the mansion in retaliation for destruction of British Canada's government buildings by American troops during the War of 1812. Reconstruction of the burned-out shell of the President's House was completed in 1817.

Tours of the executive mansion are under the jurisdiction of the National Park Service. The White House is generally open for tours on Tuesdays through Saturdays from 10 a.m. to noon, but is closed during official functions, programs, and on such holidays as Thanksgiving, Christmas, and New Year's Day. From Memorial Day through Labor Day weekend, free tickets are available at booths on the

Ellipse, just south of the White House, and are issued on a first-come, first-served basis from 8 a.m. until the day's supply runs out. During the rest of the year, no tickets are required, and visitors may go directly to the East Gate of the White House. Self-guided tours take visitors through the ground and state floors. Handicapped visitors enter through the north portico and front door, directly onto the state floor. No tickets are required for the handicapped or those accompanying them, and wheelchairs are available at the Northeast Gate on Pennsylvania Avenue.

MAINE

Saint Croix Island International Historic Site

c/o Acadia National Park
P.O. Box 177
Bar Harbor, ME 04609-0807
207-288-3338

Managed in cooperation with Canada's Department for the Environment, this 35-acre international historic site along the tidal estuary of the St. Croix River in eastern Maine protects and interprets the site of the first French colonial settlement in northern North America. The site, across the estuary from New Brunswick, Canada, comprises 6.5 acres on St. Croix Island, about 35 acres on the U.S. mainland, and about eight acres of intertidal terrain where the range between mean high and low tides is about 20 feet. In 1604, the 79 colonists attempted to establish a settlement on wooded Saint Croix Island, but an early and severe winter forced them to abandon the site and move across the Bay of Fundy to less isolated Port Royal (near today's town of Annapolis Royal, Nova Scotia).

The island subsequently served as a neutral meeting place during the War of 1812 between Britain and the United States. Although no structures remain on St. Croix Island, excavations have revealed foundations of buildings and the graves of those who perished during that difficult winter. Visitors may look across to the island from a hilltop in the site's mainland unit just off U.S. Route 1, eight miles south of Calais, Maine. A small interpretive facility tells the island's history. A picnic area is available.

Antietam National Battlefield

P.O. Box 158
Sharpsburg, MD 21782-0158
301-432-5124

This 3,255-acre national battlefield, located about 50 miles northwest of Washington, D.C., protects and interprets the site of the horrendous Battle of Antietam (or Sharpsburg) of September 17, 1862, that climaxed the first of Confederate Gen. Robert E. Lee's two attempts to extend the Civil War into the North. The battle was called "the bloodiest day of the Civil War" because it resulted in the largest number of casualties ever inflicted on a single day of the war. This defeat of Confederate troops caused Great Britain to postpone its recognition of the Confederacy, which contributed to the preservation of the Union and gave President Lincoln the opportunity to issue the Emancipation Proclamation.

On the battle day, Lee crossed the Potomac River and invaded Maryland with nearly 40,000 soldiers who battled a total of 87,000 Union troops. The bloodshed began early in the morning, with nearly 10,000 Union soldiers blasting the Southerners with "a terrific storm of shell, cannister, and musketry." The famous Texas brigade suffered a staggering loss of 82 percent of its men. Powerful attacks and counterattacks occurred throughout the morning. As one Union division rushed forward, Confederate reinforcements opened fire and in a mere 20 minutes, more than 2,000 Union casualties lay dead or wounded, while terrified survivors fled from the ghastly killing-field. Some of the Civil War's most desperately brutal slaughtering took place along a sunken farm road, subsequently named Bloody Lane. The carnage was so enormous that the lane was carpeted so thickly with the bodies of the dead that a person could easily have walked along the road without ever touching the ground. At day's end, nearly 4,000 soldiers had been killed at the Battle of Antietam, and an additional 18,000 lay wounded, several thousand of whom soon died from their injuries.

The visitor center, open daily except Thanksgiving, Christmas, and New Year's Day, provides interpretive exhibits, audiovisual programs, and publications. Interpreter-guided tours are offered, and a self-guided driving tour winds through the battlefield. At the southern end, the Snavely Ford Trail leads hikers from Burnside Bridge along the banks of Antietam Creek. Access to the battlefield from I-70 at Hagerstown is south about ten miles on State Route 65. The battlefield is about midway between Boonsboro, Maryland, and Shepherdstown, West Virginia, on State Route 34.

Catoctin Mountain Park

6602 Foxville Road
Thurmont, MD 21788-0158
301-663-9388

This 5,770-acre park in the Appalachian Mountains of northern Maryland protects an area of gently rolling, densely forested mountain scenery, along with richly varied flora and fauna and historic sites. Scenic drives and 25 miles of hiking trails wind through the woodlands of this park and adjacent Cunningham Falls State Park, leading visitors to waterfalls and rocky overlooks. The visitor center provides interpretive exhibits, programs, and publications. Seasonal interpretive activities include walks, campfire programs, cross-country skiing seminars, and talks about the history of this area. The park and visitor center are open year-round. Picnic areas and campgrounds are available in both parks. Access from Frederick, Maryland, is north 13 miles on U.S. Route 15 and entering west into Catoctin Mountain Park on State Route 77. Or from U.S. Route 30 near Gettysburg, Pennsylvania, drive south 21 miles on U.S. Route 15 to the State Route 77 entrance.

Chesapeake and Ohio Canal National Historical Park

P.O. Box 4
Sharpsburg, MD 21782-0004
301-739-4200

This 19,236-acre national historical park, extending 184.5 miles from the Potomac River tidewater to Cumberland, Maryland, protects and interprets the Chesapeake & Ohio Canal, which was constructed from 1828 to 1850. When the project was launched, promoters predicted the canal would become a vital link between the eastern seaboard and the Ohio River region. However, construction began on the Baltimore & Ohio Railroad on the same day as the start of the canal and, by the time the canal route was completed to Cumberland, the railroad was already running trains there and providing faster and cheaper service than the canal could offer. Consequently, the C&O Canal was largely obsolete before its completion. From Washington to Cumberland, it climbed more than 600 feet through 74 locks and was 60 feet wide and 30 feet deep. Periodically since the canal was built, floods and other events have heavily damaged the waterway. The most recent flooding occurred twice in 1996. Today, several stretches contain water, while others do not.

One of the scenic highlights of this park is the Great Falls, where the Potomac River plunges and cascades between the walls and boulders of rugged gorges. A trail beginning near Great Falls Tavern affords excellent views of the falls, which are especially spectacular following periods of heavy rain. The falls may also be viewed from the Virginia shore.

This park provides a nearly level towpath along the canal that is popular with hikers, bicyclists, and horseback riders. Stretches of quiet canal are enjoyed by canoeists, boaters, and anglers. Mule-towed boat rides are offered from mid-April to mid-October from Georgetown in Washington, D.C. (for information, call 202-472-4376) and from Great Falls Tavern in Maryland (call 301-299-2026). Canoe, boat, and bicycle rentals are offered at Thompson's Boat Center at the junction of the canal, Rock Creek, and the Potomac River (call 202-333-4861); Fletcher's Boathouse, just off Canal Rd. (call 202-244-0461); and Swains Lock (Lock 21) off River Rd. (State Route 190), just over two miles north of Potomac, Maryland (call 301-299-9006). Picnic areas and campgrounds are available.

The main visitor center/museum is located in the historic Great Falls Tavern, at 11710 MacArthur Blvd., Potomac, MD; 301-299-3613. It provides interpretive exhibits, pro-

grams, and publications. Other visitor centers are at 1057 Thomas Jefferson St., N.W., Washington, D.C. (202-653-5844); at 326 E. Main St., Hancock, MD (301-678-5463); and at the Western Maryland Station Center, Canal St., Cumberland, MD (301-722-8226).

Clara Barton National Historic Site

5801 Oxford Road
Glen Echo, MD 20812-1201
301-492-6245

This eight-acre national historic site located three miles northwest of Washington, DC, protects and interprets the early years of the American Red Cross and honors the memory of its founder, Clara Barton (1821–1912). During the Civil War, from 1861 to 1865, Barton volunteered to assist wounded soldiers at a number of major battles. In 1870, she began working with the International Red Cross in France and Germany; and from 1881 to 1904, she served as president of American Red Cross and assisted in disaster relief efforts.

The 38-room home provides interpretive exhibits, audiovisual programs (advance reservations required), and guided tours. A picnic area is available. The site is open daily, except Thanksgiving, Christmas, and New Year's Day. Access to the site from Washington, D.C. is by way of MacArthur Blvd., three miles from the District-Maryland line, then left onto Oxford Road and proceeding to the parking area between the house and Glen Echo Park. Access from I-495 (Capital Beltway) is by way of the Clara Barton Parkway to Glen Echo, following Glen Echo Park and Clara Barton NHS signs to Oxford Road.

Fort McHenry National Monument and Historic Shrine

End of East Fort Avenue
Baltimore, MD 21230-5393
410-962-4299

This 43-acre national monument, at the mouth of Baltimore Harbor, protects and interprets the late 18th-century, red-brick, star-shaped fort that was successfully defended by American soldiers against intense bombardment by British warships during the War of 1812. In spite of the battering assault on September 13–14, 1814, the massive structure sustained relatively little damage. Ironically, two Americans—Col. John Skinner and a young attorney, Francis Scott Key—were on board one of the British ships to negotiate the release of a hostage and witnessed the onslaught. In the dawn's early light on September 14, at the end of the 25-hour siege, Skinner and Key saw that the Stars and Stripes—the huge 42- by 30-foot American flag made by Baltimore seamstress Mary Pickersgill—was still waving above the fort. Key then jotted down a few poetic lines to describe his feelings over the triumph of the Americans who had so bravely defended Fort McHenry. He subsequently expanded his poem, which ultimately became the words of America's official national anthem, "The Star-Spangled Banner."

A visitor center provides interpretive exhibits, an audiovisual program, and publications. A self-guided walk leads visitors through the fort. During the summer, interpreters lead guided tours. Special programs are presented on Flag Day (June 14) and Defender's Day (September 7), and there are living-history reenactments. A picnic area is available. Access to the fort from I-95 is by way of the Key Highway/Fort McHenry exit 55. Follow the blue-and-green signs along Key Highway, then turn right onto Lawrence Street and left onto Fort Avenue to the monument. Access from the Inner Harbor area is by way of Light Street southbound, and following the signs as above.

Fort Washington Park

Mailing address:
c/o National Capital Parks-East
1900 Anacostia Drive, SE
Washington, DC 20020-6722
301-763-4600

This 341-acre park on the Maryland shore of the Potomac River, about six miles downstream from Washington, D.C., protects and interprets a massive, masonry military fortification that was established in 1824 to help defend the nation's capital from attack by river. When the Civil War broke out in 1861, the fort took on added significance because Virginia, just across the river, seceded from the Union and joined the Confederacy. At the time, Fort Washington was the only fortification near Washington, but an encircling network of earthen forts and artillery batteries was quickly established to enhance the city's protection. While this fort never saw military action during the Civil War, its weaponry and defenses were for many years periodically strengthened and upgraded.

Today, Fort Washington tells the story of evolving and improving military fortification strategies and technologies. A visitor center provides interpretive exhibits, an audiovisual program, and publications. On spring, summer, and autumn weekends, living-history reenactments and demonstrations are presented, portraying the Civil War era and the activities of a 19th-century U.S. Army garrison. A picnic area is available. Access to the park from I-495 (Capital Beltway) is at Exit 3, then south on Indian Head Highway (State Route 210) and right (southeast) on Fort Washington Road.

Greenbelt Park

6565 Greenbelt Road
Greenbelt, MD 20770-3207
301-344-3948

This 1,175-acre park, about four miles northeast of Washington, D.C., protects a scenic area of woodland, provides habitat for a diversity of flora and fauna, and offers a variety of outdoor recreational activities, including hiking, birdwatching, horseback riding, picnicking, and camping. A network of trails leads hikers throughout the park. These routes include the 1.2-mile Azalea Trail that connects the park's picnic areas; and the 1.4-mile Dogwood Trail, beginning and ending at a parking area on Park Central Road, that provides interpretive information on the area's ecological values and history. The six-mile perimeter trail offers opportunities for horseback riding and hiking. Information centers are located near the park entrance and near the campground. Interpreters offer guided walks and evening campfire programs. Access to the park is reached from I-495 at exit 22, then northbound on the Gladys Spellman (Baltimore-Washington) Parkway to the next exit and west on Greenbelt Road (State Route 193).

Hampton National Historic Site

535 Hampton Lane
Towson, MD 21286-1397
410-962-0688

This 62-acre national historic site near Baltimore protects and interprets an elaborate, late-18th-century mansion originally called Hampton Hall. For more than 150 years, this was the lavish home of Capt. Charles Ridgely and six generations of his prominent family. Once surrounded by a 24,000-acre estate with a complex of outbuildings, formal gardens, vineyards, orchards, extensive pastures and fields, grand trees, and prize-winning race horses, the home was served by a large number of slaves and indentured servants. The three-story mansion, which is topped by an imposing cupola, is an ostentatiously ornate takeoff from the typically more conservative Georgian architecture of the post-Revolutionary period. The interior is furnished to reflect the late 18th- to late 19th-centuries, and visitors may see many of the original Ridgely family possessions.

Tours of the mansion are offered, in addition to self-guided tours through the gardens, farm, stables, and other areas of the property. The site is open daily, except Thanksgiving, Christmas, and New Year's Day. Access from I-695 is by the exit onto Dulaney Valley Road (State Route 146) northbound toward Hampton and right onto Hampton Lane.

Monocacy National Battlefield

4801 Urbana Pike
Frederick, MD 21701-7307
301-662-3515

This 1,647-acre national battlefield, 35 miles northwest of Washington, D.C., protects and interprets the site of a Civil War battle on July 9, 1864, in which Confederate forces defeated outnumbered Union troops. However, the battle turned out to be a strategic victory, as it delayed the Southerners' daring advance toward Washington and gave the Northerners time to assemble reinforcements in a successful defense of the federal capital. The Confederates penetrated as far as Fort Stevens, in the northern part of the District of Columbia but were then easily driven back by Union soldiers, who had arrived just in time to reinforce the city's defenses. Thus, the Battle of Monocacy is also called the "Battle That Saved Washington."

The visitor center, located two-tenths-of-a-mile south of the Monocacy River on State Route 355, provides interpretive exhibits, an audiovisual program, and publications. It is open daily from Memorial Day weekend through Labor Day weekend and on Wednesdays through Sundays the rest of the year. The center is closed Thanksgiving, Christmas, and New Year's Day. A half-mile trail leads from the center, and a four-mile, self-guided drive winds through the battlefield. Access to the battlefield is three miles south of Frederick on State Route 355.

Piscataway Park

c/o National Capital Parks-East
1900 Anacostia Drive, S.E.
Washington, DC 20020-6722
301-763-4600

The 4,440-acre, six-mile stretch of land from Piscataway Creek to Marshall Hall along the Maryland shore of the Potomac River was established to protect the historic panorama across the river from George Washington's famous home, Mount Vernon, on the river's Virginia shore. The park includes the National Colonial Farm, a re-created 18th-century Tidewater farm. Living-history interpreters in period costumes take visitors on tours of the farm, which is operated by Accokeek Foundation, Inc., in cooperation with the National Park Service. The farm uses techniques representative of 18th-century farming. The farm is open on Tuesdays through Sundays, except Thanksgiving, Christmas, and New Year's Day. Also within Piscataway Park are the remains of Marshall Hall, an early 18th-century plantation. Several short self-guided nature trails wind along stretches of river shore. Picnic areas are available.

The park is open daily, except Thanksgiving, Christmas, and New Year's Day. Access to the park from I-495 (Capital Beltway) is by way of exit 3A, then south ten miles on Indian Head Highway (State Route 210) to Accokeek and onto Bryan Point Road.

Potomac Heritage National Scenic Trail

c/o C&O Canal National Historical Park
P.O. Box 4
Sharpsburg, MD 21782-0004
301-739-4200

This national scenic trail is projected to run 704 miles up the Potomac River valley from the mouth of the river to the Laurel Highlands. It includes the 17-mile Mount Vernon Trail along the George Washington Memorial Parkway in Virginia; the 184.5-mile Chesapeake & Ohio Canal towpath from Georgetown in Washington, D.C., to Cumberland, Maryland, and the 70-mile Laurel Highlands National Recreation Trail in Pennsylvania. Other segments of the trail have yet to be designated and planned.

Thomas Stone National Historic Site

6655 Rose Hill Road
Port Tobacco, MD 20677-3400
301-934-6027

This 328-acre national historic site in southern Maryland protects and interprets "Habre-de-Venture," a red-brick, Georgian-style mansion built in 1771 near Port Tobacco on the north shore of the lower Potomac River. From 1743 to 1787, this was the home of Thomas Stone, a signer of the Declaration of Independence and a delegate to the Continental Congress. The site offers self-guided and interpreter-led tours, a brief audiovisual program, and occasional special events. It is open daily, except Thanksgiving, Christmas, and New Year's Day. Access from U.S. Route 301 southbound at La Plata is right onto State Route 6 and right onto Rose Hill Road. From State Route 210 southbound from Washington, D.C., take a left onto State Route 225 eastbound and a right onto Rose Hill Road.

MASSACHUSETTS

Adams National Historic Site

P.O. Box 531, 135 Adams Street
Quincy, MA 02269-0531
617-770-1175

This 13-acre national historic site protects and interprets the home of the second and sixth presidents of the United States, John Adams and John Quincy Adams, and other members of this illustrious family. It is considered the most historic house in the United States, as it and all its furnishings consistently remained in the family. "Peacefield," as John Adams called it, or The Old House, as other family members referred to it, was originally a small building, dating from 1731, but it was expanded to twice that size by John and Abigail Adams. The site also contains the two houses in which the two presidents were born.

A visitor center provides interpretive exhibits, programs, and publications. Visitors obtain passes at the center for touring the three historic buildings, including trolley transportation from the visitor center to each house. The center is open daily, except on weekends, from November 11 through April 18. Access from Boston is on I-93 southbound to the Route 3 South exit; on Route 3, take the Washington Street exit and follow signs to the Quincy "T" subway station, where the route turns into the Burgin Parkway. At the seventh light, turn right onto Dimmock Street, proceed one block, and turn right onto Hancock Street. The visitor center is at 1250 Hancock in the Galleria at Presidents Place, with parking at the rear of the building.

Boston African American National Historic Site

46 Joy Street
Beacon Hill, MA 02114-4025
617-742-5415

This national historic site in Boston includes 14 pre-Civil War, African-American historic structures linked by the 1.6-mile Black Heritage Trail. The Augustus Saint-Gaudens memorial to Robert Gould Shaw, the white officer who led African-American troops from the North during the Civil War, is located in Boston Common across from the State House. Also notable are the oldest standing African-American church in the United States and the Museum of African American History.

The information office, located in the Abiel Smith School building at 46 Joy Street, is open five days per week, except Thanksgiving, Christmas, and New Year's Day. The Black Heritage Trail may be taken as a self-guided

73

walking tour or interpreter-guided tours, which are offered daily from Memorial Day to Labor Day and by special arrangement the rest of the year. Access from the Massachusetts Turnpike is by way of the Prudential-Copley Square exit to Stuart Street and left onto Charles Street (State Route 28) to Boston Common. Since parking may be virtually impossible in downtown Boston (there is a parking facility beneath Boston Common), visitors may prefer to take a taxi or travel by public transportation on the MBTA Red or Green line to Park Street Station.

Boston Harbor Islands National Recreation Area

408 Atlantic Ave.
Boston, MA 02110
617-223-8666

This 1,482-acre national recreation area in Boston Harbor protects 30 islands that contain a wide variety of natural and historical resources. Established in 1996, Boston Harbor Islands offers recreational activities and educational interpretation on the natural significance, Native American culture, and use of Massachusetts and Cape Cod bays. Several islands shelter historic structures, such as a 19th-century fort and Boston Light, America's first lighthouse, built in 1716. Other islands are natural sanctuaries for birds. Some of the islands offer camping, and swimming. The area is being managed in a partnership between the current managers and owners and the National Park Service.

Boston National Historical Park

Charlestown Navy Yard
Boston, MA 02129-4543
617-242-5601

This 41-acre national historical park protects, interprets, and focuses national attention on significant places and events that helped spur the American colonies toward independence from Britain. Sites include: Faneuil Hall (below Government Center, near the intersection of Congress and North streets); Old South Meeting House (310 Washington Street); Old State House (206 Washington Street); Paul Revere House (19 North Square, in Boston's

North End); Old North Church (193 State Street); Bunker Hill Monument (in Monument Square, between High and Bartlett streets, in Charlestown); and part of the Charlestown Navy Yard, where the historic frigate USS *Constitution* may be viewed. Most of the sites are connected by the 2.5-mile Freedom Trail.

The National Park Service offers interpreter-led walking tours on the downtown Boston stretch from mid-April through November. Walking the entire trail, from Boston Common to Bunker Hill, requires most of a day or parts of more than a day. A red line along the pavement leads the way for most of the route. Park visitor centers are located at 15 State Street across from the Old State House in downtown Boston and next to Dry Dock #1 near the USS *Constitution* in Charlestown. The park is open daily, except on Thanksgiving, Christmas, and New Year's Day. As parking may be virtually impossible in downtown Boston (there is a parking facility beneath Boston Common), visitors may prefer to take a taxi or public transportation.

Frederick Law Olmsted National Historic Site

99 Warren Street
Brookline, MA 02146-5998
617-566-1689

This nearly two-acre national historic site in the Boston suburb of Brookline honors the celebrated landscape architect Frederick Law Olmsted and protects and interprets "Fairsted," which was his home and office. In 1883, Olmsted moved from New York City to a farmhouse in Brookline, where he established America's first professional practice of landscape architecture. Over the years, Olmsted designed New York's Central Park, Boston's park system, and hundreds of campuses, suburban developments, estates, and other city parks. His landmark design concept was the creation of green and open spaces where people could escape city pressures and rejuvenate themselves in body and spirit.

The site provides interpretive exhibits, an audiovisual program, and publications. Visitors may tour the Olmsted office, home, and attractively landscaped grounds. The site is open Fridays through Sundays, except Christmas and New Year's Day. Access to the site from I-95 is by way of the State Route 9 East (Brookline/Boston) exit, proceeding on Route 9 to just beyond the Brookline Reservoir (on the right), turning right onto Warren Street and continuing to the site at the intersection of Warren and Dudley streets. From the Massachusetts Turnpike westbound, take the Brighton-Harvard Street exit, proceed on Harvard, turn right onto Boylston Street (State Route 9) and then left onto Warren, to the site at the intersection of Warren and Dudley streets.

John Fitzgerald Kennedy National Historic Site

**83 Beals Street
Brookline, MA 02146-3010
617-566-7937**

This national historic site, in the Boston suburb of Brookline, protects and interprets the 1917 birthplace and boyhood home of John Fitzgerald Kennedy (1917–63), the 35th president of the United States. The National Park Service offers interpretive tours of the house, and a walking tour of the surrounding neighborhood includes the house the Kennedy family moved to in 1921 and the church and schools JFK attended. The site is open daily, except Thanksgiving, Christmas, and New Year's Day. Access is by way of the Allston-Cambridge-Brighton exit from the Massachusetts Turnpike Extension, proceeding on Cambridge Street (toward Allston), and then left onto Harvard Street and left onto Beals Street.

Longfellow National Historic Site

**105 Brattle Street
Cambridge, MA 02138-3407
617-876-4491**

This two-acre national historic site protects and interprets the Georgian-style house dating from 1759 where George Washington headquartered as commander of the Continental Army during the British siege of Boston in 1775–76. The house is also where one of America's foremost 19th-century poets, Henry Wadsworth Longfellow (1807–82), lived for 45 years while teaching at Harvard. Longfellow was a profes-

sor of modern languages and a linguist who strongly believed in a multicultural America and the preservation of native languages, so it was in his house that numerous stimulating debates on social reform took place among the intelligentsia of the time.

Visitors may see Longfellow's study and the desk at which he wrote such works as "Evangeline: A Tale of Acadie" (1847), "The Song of Hiawatha" (1855), and Tales of a Wayside Inn (1863, 1872, and 1873). Interpreter-guided tours of the house are offered, and summer concerts are presented in the garden every other Sunday (weather permitting) beginning in mid-June. The site is open daily, except Thanksgiving, Christmas, and New Year's Day. Visitors wishing to avoid trying to park in busy Cambridge may park beneath Boston Common, ride the Red Line subway to Harvard Square, and walk just over a half-mile down Brattle Street to #105.

Lowell National Historical Park

**169 Merrimack Street
Lowell, MA 01852-1029
508-970-5000**

This 137-acre national historical park commemorating the history of the Industrial Revolution in America features historic 19th-century cotton textile mill complexes, more than five miles of a canal network, and housing for mill workers. Through these structures, the park illustrates the transition from a farming to a factory economy, immigrant labor history, and the development of industrial technology. A visitor center at 246 Market Street provides interpretive exhibits, an audiovisual program, and publications. In addition to self-guided touring, the park offers guided tours on foot, by trolley (for a fee), and by canal barge (for a fee) from July 1 to Columbus Day. Other exhibits presented in the park include the Working People Exhibit in the Mogan Cultural Center. The park is open daily, except Thanksgiving, Christmas, and New Year's Day. Access, from either I-495 or U.S. Route 3, is by way of the Lowell Connector, exiting onto Thorndike Street northbound and proceeding about a half-mile, and turning right onto Dutton Street to the parking area.

75

Minute Man National Historical Park

174 Liberty Street
Concord, MA 01742
508-369-6993

This 935-acre national historical park along the road between Lexington and Concord in eastern Massachusetts commemorates the events and follows part of the route of the first battle in the American Revolution, when fighting broke out between British redcoats and greatly outnumbered Massachusetts colonial militiamen and minutemen on April 19, 1775. Sites include North Bridge, the "Minute Man" statue sculpted by Daniel Chester French, colonial homes, four miles of Battle Road, and the homes of authors Louisa May Alcott and Nathaniel Hawthorne.

The park has two visitor centers. The North Bridge Visitor Center, which is open daily except Thanksgiving, Christmas, and New Year's Day, is near the reconstructed bridge across the Concord River. The Battle Road Visitor Center, which is open daily from mid-April through October, is about a mile west of Lexington Green. Both centers provide interpretive exhibits, audiovisual programs, and publications. Living-history demonstrations are presented, notably of the Battle at North Bridge, on the third Monday in April (Patriots Day, a state holiday). Access to the park from I-95 is by way of exit 30B into Lexington or from I-495 onto State Route 2 to Concord.

New Bedford Whaling National Historical Park

33 William Street
New Bedford, MA 02740

508-997-1776

This 20-acre national historical park in southeast Massachusetts commemorates whaling and its contribution to early American history. The park includes the National Historic Landmark District, the New Bedford Whaling Museum, and the schooner *Ernestina*. New Bedford is reached by either I-195 or U.S. Route 6.

Salem Maritime National Historic Site

174 Derby Street
Salem, MA 01970-5186
508-740-1660

This nine-acre national historic site along the Salem waterfront in northeast Massachusetts protects and interprets nine buildings and three wharfs that represent the late 18th- and early 19th-century maritime history of this seaport, then one of the world's busiest international shipping centers. When the American colonies declared their independence from Britain, more ship owners from Salem than from any other American port city responded to the Continental Congress's appeal for American ships to attack and disrupt British shipping and to seize weapons and supplies for use by the Continental Army. Salem privateers captured more than 400 British ships. Following the war, Salem launched its most successful period of international maritime trade, including the Orient, South Pacific, Africa, Europe, and South America. Fifty wharfs, with dozens of warehouses for storing such imports as silks, cotton, cotton fabrics, ivory, spices, coffee, and cocoa, once extended into bustling Salem Harbor. However, the shipping heyday sharply declined after the United States slapped an embargo on trade with France and Britain in 1807.

Featured at the site today are the Custom House, dating from 1819, where shipping merchants obtained permits to land cargo and paid U.S. customs taxes; the Scale House, dating from 1829, where U.S. Customs Service agents kept scales for weighing cargo on board ships; the Derby House, dating from 1762 and fronting on Derby Wharf; the West India Goods Store, dating from around 1800, a popular local retail sales outlet for imported foods and other merchandise from around the world; and the Central Wharf Warehouse, dating from 1805 and now housing the site's orientation center with interpretive exhibits, an audiovisual program, and publications. Historic structures may be visited on either self-guided or interpreter-guided tours (reservations may be required). The site is open daily, except Thanksgiving, Christmas, and New Year's Day. Access to the site from I-95 is by way of exit 26 (Lowell Street) or exit 25A (State Route 114 East) to historic downtown Salem, and then following signs to the Salem Regional

Visitor Center at 2 Liberty Street, where parking is provided. A Heritage Walking Tour leads from this center to the site's orientation center.

Saugus Iron Works National Historic Site

244 Central Street
Saugus, MA 01906-2107
617-233-0050

This eight-acre national historic site protects and interprets the location of the first integrated ironworks in North America. Operated from 1646 to 1668, the ironworks helped lay the foundation for the iron-and-steel industry in the United States. The site features the reconstructed blast furnace, forge, rolling and slitting mill, and a restored 17th-century house used as living quarters, the company office, and a place to entertain business guests. The iron-ore smelting process used large quantities of charcoal from acres of hardwood forest to fuel the blast furnace, which was in operation around the clock. The furnace's intense heat converted the ore to liquid iron, some of which was made into finished products, such as kettles, pots, and pans. Much of the iron was made into brittle, cast-iron bars, and these were then taken to the forge where they were converted to more malleable wrought iron "merchant bars." The slitting mill further processed the wrought iron—flattening the bars into "flats" and slitting them into "rod" stock for nails. In 1650, only about a dozen mills in the world had this advanced technology.

The museum provides interpretive exhibits and an audiovisual program. Publications are available in a gift shop in the visitor contact station. Self-guided and interpreter-led tours of the site are offered, and an interpretive nature trail winds along the east bank of the Saugus River. A picnic area is available. The site is open daily, except Thanksgiving, Christmas, and New Year's Day. Access from I-95 at Lynnfield is by way of Exit 43 and proceeding five miles on Walnut Street, following the brown signs to the entrance.

Springfield Armory National Historic Site

1 Armory Square
Springfield, MA 01105-1299
413-734-8551

This 55-acre national historic site protects and interprets the place where the first manufacture of small firearms for United States infantrymen occurred, from 1794 to 1968. As the United States was still fighting for its independence in 1777, Gen. George Washington chose this site above the Connecticut River for construction of the new country's first arsenal. Over the next 190 years, the original warehouse for muskets grew into one of the most important facilities for the design, development, and production of military arms in the world. Among the best-known U.S. Army firearms were the Springfield rifle (M1903) used in World War I and the M1 rifle used during World War II.

One of the armory buildings now houses a museum that presents exhibits of firearms and the history of their production. Interpretive programs and publications are available. The site is open daily, except Thanksgiving, Christmas, and New Year's Day. Access to the site from I-91 northbound is by way of Exit 4 onto Broad Street; turning right onto State Street, left onto Federal Street, and left into Springfield Technical Community College; and then proceeding on the road to the left. From I-91 southbound, take Exit 5 (Broad Street) and turn left at the bottom of the off-ramp, then left at the stoplight onto Columbus Avenue and right onto State Street; and continuing as above.

NEW HAMPSHIRE

Saint-Gaudens National Historic Site

R.R. 3, Box 73
Cornish, NH 03745-9704
603-675-2175

This 148-acre national historic site overlooking the Connecticut River valley commemorates the life and works of American sculptor Augustus Saint-Gaudens (1848-1907) and protects and interprets "Aspet"—his home, studios, and gardens, which became a center for the summer "Cornish Colony" of painters, musicians, actors, and writers. Saint-Gaudens' works include the Farragut Monument in New York City, the bronze Robert Gould Shaw and 54th Regiment Memorial on Boston Common, and the Adams Memorial in Rock Creek Church

Cemetery in Washington, D.C. Bronze casts of these sculptures are among the more than 100 of the sculptor's works displayed at this site. Visitors are offered interpretive tours. Two nature trails offer delightful walks through the property and a picnic area is available. During the summer, a concert series and art exhibits are presented in cooperation with the Saint-Gaudens Memorial. A sculptor-in-residence program is based at Ravine Studio. The site, which is open from Memorial Day weekend through October, is located on New Hampshire Route 12A at Cornish, with various access routes from I-89 and from I-91 just across the river in Vermont.

NEW JERSEY

Edison National Historic Site

Main Street and Lakeside Avenue
West Orange, NJ 07052-5515
201-736-0550

This 21-acre, two-unit site commemorates the life and accomplishments of inventor Thomas A. Edison (1847–1931) and protects and interprets the Edison research laboratories and the 23-room Victorian mansion called "Glenmont," that was Edison's home.

By the age of ten, Edison had become passionately interested in chemistry, and as a teenager, he built his own laboratory. At 22, he received from the federal government his first patent for an invention—one of more than a thousand patents issued to him over his lifetime. In the 1870s, Edison developed numerous inventions in the field of electricity, among which were the automatic repeating telegraph, phonograph, telephone transmitter, and the first reliable incandescent light bulb. In the early 1880s, Edison developed an electric power transmission system that he installed in New York City's financial district to light hundreds of his light bulbs. In 1887, he moved to new, larger research laboratories, at what is today the laboratory unit of the national historic site. It was here that the first motion-picture camera was created.

A visitor center at the laboratory unit provides interpretive exhibits, an audiovisual program, and publications. The laboratories and

Glenmont are open for interpreter-guided tours only (daily at the laboratories and Wednesdays through Sundays at the mansion). Passes for the Glenmont tours can be obtained at the visitor center. The national historic site is open daily, except Thanksgiving, Christmas, and New Year's Day. Access from I-280 westbound is by way of Exit 10 or eastbound from Exit 9 and following the signs.

Great Egg Harbor Scenic and Recreational River

c/o Northeast Area, National Park Service
200 Chestnut Street
Philadelphia, PA 19106-2818
215-597-1582

This river in southern New Jersey offers enhanced recognition for one of the major rivers within the 1.2-million-acre Pinelands National Reserve. The area includes a 129-mile stretch of the Great Egg Harbor River's beautiful, broad, meandering course, along with pine woodlands, freshwater wetlands, and saltmarsh habitat. Canoeing, kayaking, and other boating activities are popular. The Atlantic County park system provides many of the visitor facilities, such as campgrounds, interpretive programs, and trails. The river is reached from Atlantic City Expressway, U.S. Route 322, and other roads.

Morristown National Historical Park

Washington Place
Morristown, NJ 07960-4299
201-539-2016

This 1,683-acre, four-unit park in northern New Jersey protects and interprets the main encampment area of the Continental Army during much of 1777 and during the brutally severe winter of 1779–80 in the Revolutionary War. The park features the site of Fort Nonsense built in 1777, Gen. George Washington's winter headquarters in the Ford family mansion, the winter encampment at Jockey Hollow for 10,000 soldiers, and the New Jersey Brigade's winter encampment area.

The winter of 1779-80 was the worst in the 18th century, with at least 20 major snowstorms roaring through the region, repeatedly paralyzing transportation and cutting off vital supply routes for the army. The bitter cold and dampness penetrated the soldiers' log huts, while insufficient clothing, bedding, and food caused immense suffering, leading the morale of the troops and officers to sink to the depths of despair. The Continental Congress, remaining unconvinced that the army faced a severe crisis, refused to act to alleviate the hardships. In desperation, Washington appealed to the state of New Jersey and its counties for assistance. New Jersey responded generously and, in his words, "saved the army from dissolution, or starving." On June 23, 1780, the Continentals clashed with the British redcoats and forced them to retreat—thus ending the long ordeal that might have resulted in the British forces winning the war without ever firing a shot.

The visitor center is at the Jockey Hollow Encampment unit and provides interpretive exhibits, audiovisual programs, and publications. Roads loop through this area of the park with numerous interpretive stops. To the northeast of Jockey Hollow, Western Avenue leads to the Fort Nonsense unit; from there visitors reach the Washington Headquarters & Museum unit by continuing on Western Ave., turning right onto Washington St. and left onto Morris St. at Morristown Green. All routes between the park units are well marked. Guided tours of the mansion are offered. All buildings are closed on Thanksgiving, Christmas, and New Year's Day, and some are closed during the winter. The park also includes 27 miles of hiking trails, some of which are open to horseback riding. Access to the park from I-287 southbound is by way of Exit 36 to reach the Washington Headquarters unit and Exit 26B to the Jockey Hollow unit. From I-287 northbound, take the Route 202/N. Maple Avenue exit and then Exit 36A to Washington Headquarters.

NEW YORK

Castle Clinton National Monument

Manhattan Sites, National Park Service
26 Wall Street
New York, NY 10005-1907
212-344-7220

This one-acre national monument in Battery Park at the southern tip of Manhattan protects and interprets a structure dating from 1811 that was one of a number of fortified military installations established to defend the city and its harbor against possible British attack during the War of 1812. While the fort was never engaged in military action, it subsequently served as a public entertainment facility and an immigration processing depot for roughly eight million prospective U.S. citizens from 1855 to 1890. The monument, which is open daily, except Thanksgiving, Christmas, and New Year's Day, provides interpretive exhibits, programs, and publications. Access is by subway, bus, or taxi.

Eleanor Roosevelt National Historic Site

519 Albany Post Road
Hyde Park, NY 12538-1997
914-229-9115

This 180-acre national historic site protects and interprets Val-Kill Cottage, where First Lady Eleanor Roosevelt came to escape the trials of her busy life. For many years, this property was her personal retreat, but it later became her home and a peaceful place to entertain guests and foreign dignitaries. It also functioned as a place to promote local craftsworkers making furniture, pewter items, and weaving through Val-Kill Industries. The pastoral setting includes woodland, fields, and ponds. The National Park Service offers an audiovisual program and interpreter-guided tours of the cottage. The site is open daily from May to October and on weekends during the rest of the year. It is closed on Thanksgiving, Christmas, and New Year's Day. Access is two miles east of the Home of Franklin D. Roosevelt National Historic Site on U.S. Route 9G. A free shuttle is available from the Roosevelt Home to Val-Kill Cottage.

Federal Hall National Memorial

Manhattan Sites, National Park Service
26 Wall Street
New York, NY 10005-1907
212-825-6888

This national memorial at the corner of Wall and Nassau streets in lower Manhattan celebrates the site of an earlier structure built in

1703 as City Hall. When the U.S. Congress initially chose New York as the nation's capital, that building was enlarged, becoming Federal Hall. It was here that George Washington took the oath of office as the first president of the United States on April 30, 1789. Congress met in that building from 1785 to 1790 and adopted the Bill of Rights in 1789. After the national government was moved to Philadelphia for a decade and then to Washington, D.C., the original Federal Hall fell into disrepair and was torn down in 1812. The present Greek-Revival structure, dating from 1942, features a large bronze statue of George Washington. The National Park Service offers interpretive exhibits and audiovisual programs on Washington and the history of Federal Hall. The memorial is open on Mondays through Fridays, except Thanksgiving, Christmas, and New Year's Day. Access is best by subway, bus, or taxi.

Fire Island National Seashore

120 Laurel Street
Patchogue, NY 11772-3596
516-289-4810

This 19,578-acre, 32-mile-long national seashore off the south shore of Long Island protects an ecologically rich area of popular surf-pounded beaches, wind-sculpted sand dunes, picturesque groves of pines, hidden oak woodlands, saltmarsh, expanses of Moriches and Great South bays, and the Sunken Forest—an intriguing place of holly, sassafras, and tupelo nestled behind sand dunes. The seashore contains the only federally designated wilderness area in the state of New York. Activities include swimming, sunbathing, hiking, birdwatching, picnicking, camping, boating, fishing, and, in part of the seashore, public hunting during the designated season. A separate unit of the seashore protects and interprets the historic William Floyd Estate, a 612-acre property that was the home of a signer of the Declaration of Independence. Guided tours are offered of the estate from April through October; call 516-399-2030.

Among the many species of birds found at the seashore are herons, egrets, shorebirds, waterfowl, American woodcock, gulls and terns, black skimmer, and numerous songbirds. Mammals include whitetail deer and foxes. Of the rich variety of trees and other plantlife are pitch pine, eastern red cedar, sassafras, oaks (swamp white, northern red, bear, and scarlet), black cherry, beach plum, downy serviceberry (shadblow), black tupelo, American holly, red maple, northern bayberry, huckleberry, blackberry, blueberry, wild rose, sumac, wild fox grape, catbrier, poison ivy, beach pea, sea rocket, seablite, and glasswort.

Visitor centers, located at South Point West, Watch Hill, and Sailors Haven, provide information and interpretive exhibits. The seashore offers a number of hiking trails/ boardwalks, including self-guided interpretive routes at Smith Point West, Watch Hill, and Sailors Haven. A primitive campground is located at Watch Hill, for which reservations are required; call 516-597-6633. Marinas, snack bars, and other facilities are located at Watch Hill and Sailors Haven. The National Park Service warns visitors to swim only where lifeguards are stationed at Watch Hill and Sailors Haven and cautions hikers to be alert for ticks, which may carry the bacteria that causes Lyme disease, and for poison ivy, which is abundant in some places. Access to Fire Island is by way of William Floyd Parkway (State Route 46) to Smith Point West and by the Robert Moses Causeway to the Lighthouse Area. From May to November, ferries run to Watch Hill, from the Fire Island National Seashore Ferry Terminal near seashore headquarters (located south of Route 27A by way of West Avenue), and to Sailors Haven, from the end of Foster Avenue (south of Route 27A). The William Floyd Estate unit is reached north from William Floyd Parkway (State Route 46), between Route 27A and Smith Point West.

Fort Stanwix National Monument

112 East Park Street
Rome, NY 13440-5816
315-336-2090

This 15-acre national monument in central upstate New York protects and interprets the site of an unsuccessful siege in August 1777 by 1,700 British soldiers, loyalists, and allied Indians against an 800-man American garrison during the Revolutionary War. The attack upon American-held Fort Stanwix, formally held by the British, was to have been part of a broader British military strategy to take control of the Lake Champlain-Hudson River corridor between New York City and Canada, thereby splitting apart the northern American colonies of New York and New England. However, this plan was foiled.

The national monument features the reconstructed log-and earth fortification. A visitor center, interpretive exhibits, and publications sales are located in various parts of the complex. From May to September, living-history reenactments are presented. The monument is open daily, except Thanksgiving, Christmas, and New Year's Day. Access from the New York Thruway (I-90) is by way of either Exit 32 or 33 and proceeding north into downtown Rome.

Gateway National Recreation Area

**Floyd Bennett Field, Building 69
Brooklyn, NY 11234-7097
718-338-3687**

This 26,601-acre national recreation area in and around New York Harbor in New York and New Jersey protects sandy beaches, sand dunes, wooded uplands, a holly forest, salt marsh and other wildlife habitat, urban outdoor recreational facilities, and historic fortifications and airfields. The area's three main parts are: the Jamaica Bay/Breezy Point Unit in New York, featuring the historic Floyd Bennett Field, Jacob Riis Park's historic bathhouse, and the former harbor-defense installation, Fort Tilden; the Staten Island Unit in New York, featuring Great Kills Park, the historic military airfield, Miller Field, and Fort Wadsworth; and the Sandy Hook Unit in New Jersey, featuring historic Fort Hancock and Sandy Hook Lighthouse.

Visitor activities include a wide range of recreational pursuits, such as swimming on lifeguard-protected beaches, sunbathing, tennis, baseball, softball, soccer, football, cricket, miniature golf, kite-flying, bicycling, horseback riding, boating, fishing, hiking, birdwatching, ranger-led walks, environmental education programs, and special summer cultural events. The area is open daily until dusk, and a complete range of services is provided from Memorial Day through September. Fast-food services are available in all of the main units. The visitor center at Jamaica Bay National Wildlife Refuge is open daily, except Christmas and New Year's Day. For information on access by automobile or public transit, call these numbers: for Jamaica Bay/Breezy Point, 718-318-4300; for Staten Island, 718-351-7921; and for Sandy Hook, 908-872-5970.

General Grant National Memorial

**122nd Street and Riverside Drive
New York, NY 10027-3703
212-666-1640**

This three-quarter-acre national memorial at Riverside Drive and West 122nd Street at the northern end of Manhattan features the largest mausoleum in America. Also known as "Grant's Tomb," the memorial commemorates Ulysses S. Grant, the celebrated Union commander who helped bring the Civil War to an end and who subsequently served as the 18th president of the United States from 1869 to 1877. President Grant also played a role in conservation history as, on March 1, 1872, he signed into law the bill establishing Yellowstone as the world's first national park. Interpretive exhibits and talks are presented at the memorial. It is open on Wednesdays through Sundays, but is closed Thanksgiving, Christmas, and New Year's Day and certain Wednesdays that follow a national holiday on Monday or Tuesday. Access is by way of the Henry Hudson Parkway, with parking near the memorial.

Hamilton Grange National Memorial

**287 Convent Avenue
New York, NY 10031-6302
212-825-6990**

This national memorial protects and interprets the home of Alexander Hamilton (1755–1804), America's first secretary of the treasury. Hamilton built this country home for his family and named it after his grandfather's estate in Scotland. The National Park Service is presently carrying out renovations of this structure. For information about reopening and access, call 212-264-4456.

Home of Franklin D. Roosevelt National Historic Site

519 Albany Post Road
Hyde Park, NY 12538-1997
914-229-9115

This 290-acre national historic site overlooking the Hudson River protects and interprets the spacious mansion, presidential library, and grounds of Franklin Delano Roosevelt, 32nd president of the United States. Roosevelt was born and spent most of his life in residence at "Springwood," which he called his "Summer White House" during his presidency. In 1921, the year after making an unsuccessful bid for the vice-presidency, Roosevelt was stricken with polio that paralyzed his legs. With great personal courage and perseverance, he learned to walk with braces and a cane—determined to get on with his life. In 1928 and again in 1930, he was elected governor of New York State.

After being elected to the presidency in 1932, Roosevelt sought and obtained emergency powers to help the country rise from the devastating financial impacts of the Great Depression, following the stock-market crash of 1929. He proclaimed the New Deal and initiated numerous federally funded projects, including the Civilian Conservation Corps (CCC), designed to provide jobs and help put America back to work—thereby fueling the nation's economy. As governor and subsequently as president, he frequently returned to his Hyde Park home for respite from the demands of public life. President Roosevelt was elected to an unprecedented four terms and died in office at the age of 63. Both he and his wife, Eleanor, are buried in the Rose Garden.

In addition to tours of the mansion, interpretive exhibits are presented in the library, and the Tourist Information Center provides publications. The site is open daily, except on Tuesdays and Wednesday from November through March and Thanksgiving, Christmas, and New Year's Day. Access to the site is by way of U.S. Route 9, just north of Poughkeepsie in Hyde Park.

Martin Van Buren National Historic Site

P.O. Box 545
Kinderhook, NY 12106-0545
518-758-9689

This 39-acre national historic site protects and interprets "Lindenwald," the elegant retirement home of Martin Van Buren, who served as eighth president of the United States from 1837 to 1841. Guided tours of the mansion are offered, and the visitor center provides interpretive exhibits, programs, and publications. The site is open daily from mid-April through October, and is closed on Mondays and Tuesdays from November 1 through December 5 and on Thanksgiving, Christmas, and New Year's Day. Access is two miles south of Kinderhook on State Route 9H. From I-90 at the U.S. Route 9 exit, drive south about five miles on State Route 9 to Kinderhook and two miles on State Route 9H.

North Country National Scenic Trail

National Park Service
700 Rayovac Drive, Suite 100
Madison, WI 53711
608-264-5610

This national scenic trail extends 3,200 miles, from Crown Point, New York, westward through New York's Adirondack Mountains, Pennsylvania, Ohio, Michigan, Wisconsin, and Minnesota, to the Missouri River in North Dakota. The trail runs through Pictured Rocks National Lakeshore in Michigan's Upper Peninsula. Approximately half the trail is currently open to the public for hiking, cross-country skiing, and (in a few places) horseback riding.

Sagamore Hill National Historic Site

20 Sagamore Hill Road
Oyster Bay, NY 11771-1899
516-922-4788

This 83-acre national historic site on the north shore of Long Island protects and interprets "Sagamore Hill," the large estate that was the home of Theodore Roosevelt, the 26th president of the United States who served from 1901 to 1909. This substantial home reflects the enormous drive of a man who cared passionately about life and who derived immense inspiration from the natural environment. As president, he committed the power of his office to conserving the forests, wildlife, and other natural resources of America at a time when unbridled exploitation and profligate waste were the rule of the day. Many new national parks and national forests and the first national monument were established during his administration.

Guided tours of Roosevelt's home are offered, and Old Orchard Home, built by President Roosevelt's son, General Theodore Roosevelt, Jr., provides interpretive exhibits, an audiovisual program, and publications. The site is open daily, except Thanksgiving, Christmas, and New Year's Day. Access from the Long Island Expressway is by way of Exit 41 or from the Northern State Parkway by Exit 35 and north on State Route 106 to Oyster Bay. At the third stoplight in town, turn right onto E. Main Street and east three miles on Cove Neck Road.

Saint Paul's Church National Historic Site

897 South Columbus Avenue
Mount Vernon, NY 10550-5018
914-667-4116

This six-acre national historic site protects and interprets this 18th-century church that is associated with the struggle for freedom of speech and the press in colonial America. A week after the first recorded U.S. political election between candidates of opposing political parties, the New York Weekly Journal published a detailed account of corruption by the candidate for Westchester County assemblymen, who had previously been appointed as county sheriff by the British governor of the colony of New York. The sheriff and governor's choice lost the election to William Morris of the newly formed political action group, "The People's Party." In retaliation for the newspaper article, the governor ordered the newspaper publisher, John Peter Zenger, arrested, jailed, and tried for what he viewed as libelous writings. Zenger's defense was that his writings were "notoriously" factual and that he had the right to publish the information. A jury found him innocent.

This landmark trial and verdict set a significant precedent that led to the protection of the press from governmental interference in New York and which provided a strong reason for nationally ensuring freedom of the press, as subsequently embodied in the First Amendment of the Bill of Rights. The existing stone church building, replacing the earlier one of wood,

was completed in 1787. The Bill of Rights Museum occupies the former parish hall.

Visitors may tour the church, museum, and cemetery; publications are available in the museum's gift shop. The site is open on Saturday afternoons, except when a Saturday is prior to a national holiday on the following Monday; is open by appointment on Tuesdays through Fridays; and is closed on Thanksgiving, Christmas, and New Year's Day. Access from the New England Thruway (I-95) northbound is by way of the Conner Street exit. Turn left onto Conner Street and proceed one stoplight; then turn left and continue on what becomes S. Columbus Avenue (State Route 22) to the site.

Saratoga National Historical Park

648 Route 32
Stillwater, NY 12170-1604
518-664-9821

This 3,392-acre national historical park on the bank of the Hudson River in eastern New York State protects and interprets the site of the American patriots' stunning defeat of British troops in 1777—a victory that became the turning point in the Revolutionary War. On September 19, a force of 4,000 British soldiers attacked 9,000 American troops. With powerful artillery, the Americans had strongly fortified the heights and earth-and-log redoubts that commanded the Hudson River and river road. When the British advanced in three columns against the American position, a bloody battle raged for more than three hours. Just as the British forces were beginning to wither and fall back under the deadly pounding, more than 500 German troops arrived in time to prevent the defeat of the British, who soon withdrew.

On October 7, the British forces mounted a second attack. But since the initial battle, American troop strength had swelled to around 13,000 men, and they now launched a series of counterattacks that soon forced the British to fall back and then retreat under the cover of darkness to the Great Redoubt—their earth-and-log fortification above the Hudson. The next night, the British forces retreated farther to the north, to the town of Saratoga, where they were quickly surrounded by the American army. In surrendering on October 17, the British commander pledged that his troops would be sent back across the Atlantic Ocean, never again to take up arms against America. In these battles, the British suffered 1,000 casualties, while the Americans lost fewer than half that number.

The visitor center, open daily except Thanksgiving, Christmas, and New Year's Day, provides interpretive exhibits, programs, and publications. From there, a nine-mile, self-guided interpretive drive winds through the park. Tour roads are open from early April through November. Hiking trails include the four-mile Wilkinson National Recreation Trail beginning at the visitor center. Visitors are cautioned to be alert for poison ivy, which is common in the park. In winter, the trails become excellent (ungroomed) cross-country skiing routes. Two picnic areas are available. Access to the park is about 30 miles north of Albany on U.S. Route 4.

Statue of Liberty National Monument

**Liberty Island
New York, NY 10004-1467
212-363-7621**

This 58-acre, two-unit national monument on Liberty and Ellis islands in New York Harbor protects and interprets the colossal, 151-foot-tall Statue of Liberty and the Ellis Island Immigration Museum. This museum honors the memory and courage of 12 million immigrants who passed through the processing and holding facilities on Ellis Island from 1892 to 1954. The statue, "Liberty Enlightening the World," was conceived as the embodiment of political freedom and as a gift in 1886 of international friendship from France to the United States. It has become a universal beacon of hope for people around the world who yearn for freedom from oppression and persecution. It is also a reminder to Americans of the cherished freedoms and opportunities they are privileged to enjoy.

A museum, with interpretive exhibits, is located within old Fort Wood. Visitors may view New York Harbor from the promenade, colonnade, and higher levels atop the pedestal. A 22-story climb inside the statue offers an unforgettable view from windows in the crown, but visitors are cautioned not to underestimate the stamina required to climb the 162 steps from pedestal to crown. The Main Building on Ellis Island provides food service for visitors, along with a gift shop offering publications and other items relating to the immigration theme. Access to the national monument is by way of the Circle Line-Statue of Liberty Ferry that runs daily at regular intervals from Battery Park at the southern tip of Manhattan and from Liberty Park in New Jersey.

Theodore Roosevelt Birthplace National Historic Site

**28 East 20th Street
New York, NY 10003-1399
212-260-1616**

This national historic site features the birthplace of Theodore Roosevelt, who served as president of the United States from 1901 to 1909. Roosevelt was born on October 27, 1858, in a typical New York brownstone on a quiet, tree-lined street in New York City's then most fashionable residential district. The Roosevelt family lived there until 1872; then the building was demolished in 1916 but was reconstructed and rededicated in 1923. Victorian period furnishings were provided by the president's widow and sisters. The site is closed on Mondays and Tuesdays, as well as on national holidays, such as Thanksgiving, Christmas, and New Year's Day. Access is by way of the 14th and 23rd street subway stops (N, R, and #6 lines) or by taxi.

Theodore Roosevelt Inaugural National Historic Site

**641 Delaware Avenue
Buffalo, NY 14202-1079
716-884-0095**

This national historic site commemorates the place where Vice President Theodore Roosevelt took the oath of office as the 26th president of the United States on September 14, 1901. Immediately after the assassination of President William McKinley, the swearing-in ceremony was held in the library of the Ansley and Mary Wilcox home. As a pioneer in the development of social work and civil service reform, Wilcox welcomed important local and national figures to his home. The site is open daily, except on Saturdays in January through March. Interpretive exhibits, a slide program, and tours are provided, and a variety of educational lectures and other activities are offered. Special events include a reenactment of the September 14 inaugural ceremony and a Victorian Christmas celebration. Access to the site from downtown Buffalo is one mile north on Delaware Avenue.

Vanderbilt Mansion National Historic Site

519 Albany Post Road
Hyde Park, NY 12538-1997
914-229-9115

This 211-acre national historic site overlooking the Hudson River protects and interprets this palatial, 19th-century, Italian Renaissance-style mansion that was built from 1899 to 1903 by Frederick W. Vanderbilt. The house is an outstanding example of the opulent estates of millionaires who amassed enormous fortunes during America's rapid, late 19th-century industrial expansion. The visitor center located in the pavilion near the mansion provides interpretive exhibits and an audiovisual program. Tours of the mansion and grounds are offered. The site is open daily from April through October and on Thursdays through Mondays from November through March; it is closed Thanksgiving, Christmas, and New Year's Day. Access to Vanderbilt Mansion is by way of U.S. Route 9, eight miles north of Poughkeepsie or 18 miles south of Rhinebeck.

Women's Rights National Historical Park

136 Fall Street
Seneca Falls, NY 13148-1517
315-568-2991

This seven-acre, several unit national historical park in western New York State commemorates the long struggle for women's rights and equality. In Seneca Falls, the park protects and interprets a number of historic properties, including the home of Elizabeth Cady Stanton, a writer and activist who led the formal beginning of the women's equal rights movement at the First Women's Rights Convention in August 1848. It also features the remains of the Wesleyan Methodist Chapel where that convention with 300 participants was held. In Waterloo, the park includes the M'Clintock House, in which the Declaration of Sentiments was written, and the privately owned Hunt House in which the equal rights leadership met to plan the convention.

At the time of the First Women's Rights Convention, unmarried women were only permitted to earn a living as teachers, seamstresses, mill workers, or domestics and were not allowed to attend college, hold public office, speak in public, or vote in political elections. Married women were barred from owning their own property, filing lawsuits, entering into contracts, divorcing an abusive husband, or gaining custody of their children. The initial group of equal rights advocates, including Elizabeth Cady Stanton, Lucretia Mott, Martha Wright, Mary Ann M'Clintock, and Jane Hunt, assembled a list of grievances patterned after the Declaration of Independence. The Declaration of Sentiments signed by convention delegates read: "We hold these truths to be self-evident: that all men and women are created equal."

The visitor center at 136 Fall Street (U.S. Route 20) in Seneca Falls provides interpretive exhibits, an orientation film, videos, and publications. Adjacent to the center is Declaration Park, in which a granite water-wall displays the inscribed words of the Declaration of Sentiments. Just east of this park are the remains of Wesleyan Chapel. The restored, white-clapboard Stanton House, at 32 Washington Street, is open for guided tours during the summer and for tours on a limited basis during the rest of the year. In Waterloo, the two-story, red-brick M'Clintock House is located on East William Street between Virginia and Church streets and the two-story, red-brick Hunt House (not open to the public) is located on East Main Street (U.S. Route 20). The park is open daily, except Thanksgiving, Christmas, and New Year's Day. Access to the visitor center from the New York Thruway (I-90) is by way of Exit 41, then four miles south on State Route 414 and left (east) two miles on U.S. Route 20 to the junction of Fall and Clinton streets.

Allegheny Portage Railroad National Historic Site

P.O. Box 189
Cresson, PA 16630-0189
814-886-6100

This 1,249-acre national historic site in the Allegheny Mountains of west-central Pennsylvania protects and interprets the remains of a passenger and freight railroad portage constructed between 1831 and 1834. By linking two major stretches of the Pennsylvania Mainline Canal, this portage slashed travel time between Philadelphia and Pittsburgh from three weeks to only four days.

The portage worked via a series of rail incline planes stairstepped a thousand feet up each side of the Allegheny Mountain Range. Passengers and freight were initially transferred from canal boats to railroad cars to cross the mountain, but the system was soon simplified with the invention of sectionalized packet-boats that were floated onto flatbed railroad cars. According to the National Park Service: "[The boats' sections] were hauled from the water by stationary steam engines, then pulled by locomotives at about 15 mph over the long grade to the first incline. In a small shed at the foot of the incline, workers hitched three cars at a time, each with a load averaging 7,000 pounds, to the continuous cable that moved over rollers between the rails. This cable was pulled at about 4 mph by a stationary steam engine beneath a large shed at the top of the incline. . . . Five of these inclines carried the cars to the summit." The portage was made obsolete by completion of the Pennsylvania Railroad's main line across the state in 1854 and was abandoned three years later.

The visitor center provides interpretive exhibits, an introductory film, a full-scale model of a steam locomotive used on the portage, and publications. Living-history demonstrations and other interpretive programs are offered during the summer months. Interpretive boardwalks and trails lead from the vicinity of the visitor center and historic Lemon House, dating from the 1830s, which offered refreshments to portage passengers. A picnic area is also available. Access to the site from U.S. Route 22 is by way of the Gallitzin exit, 12 miles to the west of Altoona or a mile east of Cresson.

Delaware Water Gap National Recreation Area

Bushkill, PA 18324-9410
717-588-2451

This 67,191-acre national recreation area encompasses a relatively unaltered 40-mile stretch of the Delaware River in northeast Pennsylvania and adjacent New Jersey. It protects a varied landscape containing densely forested, rugged mountain terrain, as well as farmland, streams, waterfalls, ponds, and the scenic Delaware Water Gap, where the river has carved a dramatic S-turn through Kittatiny Mountain. Activities include swimming, boating, canoeing, rafting, fishing, hiking, bird-watching, and public hunting in part of the area during the designated season. Hiking trails, including a 25-mile segment of the Appalachian Trail, lead throughout the area, and picnic areas and campgrounds are available. Canoeists on extended trips may camp one night at primitive campsites along the river.

Two visitor centers provide interpretive displays, audiovisual programs, and publications. Kittatiny Point Visitor Center in New Jersey is open daily from May through October and on weekends from November through April. The Dingman Falls Visitor Center in Pennsylvania is open seasonally. Interpreter-guided walks, evening programs, and children's programs are offered during July and August. At Millbrook Village, a recreated farming village that is open seasonally, the National Park Service sponsors craft demonstrations during Millbrook Days, an annual, two-day cultural event celebrating 19th-century lifestyles held in the first full week of October. Access to the national recreation area is by way of U.S. Route 209 in Pennsylvania.

Edgar Allan Poe National Historic Site

532 North 7th Street
Philadelphia, PA 19123-3502
215-597-8780

This national historic site commemorates the life and writings of American author, poet, editor, and critic Edgar Allan Poe (1809-49). The site features the three-story, red-brick cottage where he and his wife briefly resided, from 1843 to 1844, before moving to New York City. It was here that Poe achieved his greatest success as editor, critic, and author of murder mysteries and other stories, including "The Gold Bug" and "The Black Cat." The site also protects two neighboring buildings that provide interpretive exhibits and an audiovisual program. The site, which is open daily except Thanksgiving, Christmas, and New Year's Day, is just north of Spring Garden Street on 7th Street, about a mile north of Independence Hall.

Eisenhower National Historic Site

97 Taneytown Road
Gettysburg, PA 17325-1080
717-338-9114

This 690-acre national historic site protects and interprets the home of Dwight David Eisenhower, who was supreme Allied commander in Europe in World War II, known best for leading the successful invasion of Normandy in 1944, and 34th president of the United States, serving from 1953 to 1961. The Eisenhower Administration ended the Korean War, launched America's space program, and created the interstate highway system. The Gettysburg farm was a cherished retreat for the president and his wife, Mamie, and a peaceful place to entertain guests and foreign dignitaries, such as Britain's Winston Churchill, France's Charles De Gaulle, and the Soviet Union's Nikita Khrushchev.

Visitors begin interpretive tours from the Eisenhower Tour Center in the lobby of the Gettysburg National Military Park visitor center. From there, a shuttle service takes visitors to the farm, where a brief introductory program and interpretive exhibits are provided, prior to a self-guided tour of the home and grounds. The site is open daily from April through October. It is closed on Mondays and Tuesdays from November through March; on Thanksgiving, Christmas, and New Year's Day; and for four weeks during the winter. Access to the Gettysburg National Military Park's visitor center is by way of Taneyville

Road (State Route 134), near its junction with U.S. Business Route 15.

Fort Necessity National Battlefield

The National Pike
1 Washington Parkway
Farmington, PA 15437-9514
724-329-5512

This 902-acre national battlefield in southwest Pennsylvania protects and interprets the site of a fort where the first major battle of the seven-year French and Indian War between Britain and France occurred. The claim to this upper Ohio River area, part of an extensive interior region of North America, was in dispute between the two European powers. The English colony of Virginia was claiming the region at the same time French fur trappers and military troops were advancing southward from their fort at Niagara Falls.

The clash took place in 1754 in the vast forested wilderness that extended westward from the Allegheny Mountains. Virginia's colonial governor dispatched a small force of militiamen under the command of then Lt.Col. George Washington to negotiate a solution. When his efforts were unsuccessful, on May 28, Washington and 40 of his recruits marched to a glen (later named Jumonville Glen) where a 32-man force of French soldiers was camped. Washington's men opened fire and so caught the French off guard that they surrendered after a mere 15 minutes of combat. Casualties totaled ten Frenchman to only one Virginian. Washington and his men then returned to an opening in the forest, called Great Meadows, and built Fort Necessity—a small circular fortification with log stockade, storehouse, and defensive trenches. When the anticipated retaliatory attack came on July 3 during a heavy rainstorm, Washington's small number of recruits were no match for the 600 Frenchmen and their 100 Indian allies. A fierce and bloody, eight-hour battle led to Washington's surrender—the only military surrender in his distinguished military career. This battle began the war that ultimately gave Britain control of the vast region west of the Appalachian Mountains.

The visitor center, open daily except Christmas, provides interpretive exhibits, a brief slide show, and publications. From there a short path leads to the reconstructed fort, where living history reenactments are presented during the summer. The Jumonville Glen unit of the national battlefield, which is closed from November to mid-April, offers self-guided interpretive trails through this scenic area. The park also features the Mount Washington Tavern, a historic, early 19th-century stagecoach stop that now presents interpretive exhibits. Access to the battlefield visitor center from Uniontown is 11 miles east on U.S. Route 40.

Friendship Hill National Historic Site

R.D. 1, Box 149A
Point Marion, PA 15474
724-725-9190

This 674-acre national historic site overlooking the Monongahela River in southwest Pennsylvania protects and interprets the brick-and-stone Gallatin House that was the country estate of Swiss-born Albert Gallatin (1761-1849), who was secretary of the treasury from 1801 to 1813 during the Jefferson and Madison presidential administrations. Gallatin was a scholar, financier, and skillful diplomat who is remembered for his important roles in purchasing the vast Louisiana Territory from France and in negotiating an end to the War of 1812.

The house is open daily, except on Christmas, for self-guided tours. Interpretive exhibits and programs on Gallatin's life and accomplishments are presented at the house, and interpreter-led tours are offered in the summer. Ten miles of hiking trails wind through the surrounding property. Picnic facilities are available. Access to the site from Point Marion, near the Pennsylvania-West Virginia line, is three miles north on State Route 166.

Hopewell Furnace National Historic Site

2 Mark Bird Lane
Elverson, PA 19520-9505
610-582-8773

This 848-acre national historic site in southeast Pennsylvania protects and interprets an outstanding example of the hundreds of rural iron plantations in 19th-century America. With

some interruptions, Hopewell Furnace was operated from 1771 to 1883. Soon after its founding, this furnace provided George Washington's Continental Army with cannon, shot, and shell during the Revolutionary War. The postwar depression and a flood in 1786 put the ironmaster, Mark Bird, out of business, but the operation was restarted in 1816. From then until 1844, Hopewell Furnace produced tens of thousands of iron and wood-burning stoves, as well as kettles, pots, and pans. The furnace was kept roaring 24 hours per day, with tenant workers laboring in 12-hour shifts, and the equivalent of an acre of hardwood forest, converted into charcoal, consumed daily. Ultimately, Hopewell and other small furnaces were unable to compete against technological advances, and this one closed in 1883.

The visitor center provides interpretive exhibits, an audiovisual program, and publications. Visitors may tour such historic structures as the charcoal-fired blast furnace, casthouse, ironmaster's house, blacksmith shop, company store, and charcoal cooling shed. Living-history demonstrations are presented during the summer. Hiking trails wind through the northern part of the site, connecting with trails in French Creek State Park. The site is open daily, except on national holidays. Access to the site is 16 miles from the Pennsylvania Turnpike (I-76) westbound by way of Exit 23 (Downingtown), then north on State Route 100, west (left) onto State Route 23, and right (north) onto State Route 345. Visitors may also drive ten miles from the Pennsylvania Turnpike eastbound by way of Exit 22 (Morgantown), then east on State Route 23 and north (left) on State Route 345.

Johnstown Flood National Memorial

c/o Allegheny Portage Railroad
National Historic Site
P.O. Box 189
Cresson, PA 16630-0189
814-495-4643

This 164-acre site in southwest Pennsylvania memorializes the death and destruction caused in Johnstown by a break in the South Fork Dam on May 31, 1889. Following heavy rains, the dam's failure unleashed 20 million tons of water that devastated this riverside steel company town and killed 2,209 people. After the flood, the American Red Cross, under the leadership of Clara Barton, performed its first major disaster relief program. The site is open daily, except Christmas. The visitor center provides interpretive exhibits, an audiovisual program, and publications, and the Great Flood is commemorated annually at the end of May with special programs. Several self-guided interpretive trails lead through the area, including the South Fork Abutment Trail. A picnic area is available. Access to the memorial from Johnstown is northeast approximately ten miles on U.S. Route 219 to the Saint Michael exit; then east 1.5 miles on State Route 869, left onto Lake Road, and continuing 1.5 miles to the visitor center.

Middle Delaware National Scenic River

c/o Delaware Water Gap National Recreation Area
River Road
Bushkill, PA 18324-9410
717-588-2435

This 1,973-acre national scenic river in northeastern Pennsylvania and adjacent New Jersey protects part of the Delaware Water Gap National Recreation Area, where the Delaware River makes an S-turn in the scenic Delaware Water Gap through Kittatiny Mountain. Activities include swimming, boating, canoeing, rafting, fishing, hiking, and birdwatching. (For details, see the Delaware Water Gap National Recreation Area entry.)

Steamtown National Historic Site

150 South Washington Avenue
Scranton, PA 18503-2018
717-340-5200

This 62-acre national historic site interprets the century of steam railroading history in America. The site features the historic Delaware, Lackawanna & Western Railroad switching yard, including the locomotive maintenance shop, a 13-stall roundhouse, and an older three-stall section of roundhouse. The National Park Service has assembled and is restoring a collection of 28 steam locomotives and nearly 75 passenger, freight, and other railroad cars.

The visitor center and theater present interpretive exhibits and programs. Guided tours are offered of the main roundhouse, in which steam engines are being maintained. The site also contains a Railroad History Museum, where visitors may learn about the many people who ran the trains—engineers, dining-car chefs, stewards, porters, and ticket agents. From spring through autumn, steam-train excursions are offered, for which reservations are advised; call 717-340-5204. The site is open daily, except Thanksgiving, Christmas, and New Year's Day. Access from I-81 is at Exit 53, proceeding on the Central Scranton Expressway, to the first traffic light, and turning left and continuing seven blocks to the site.

Thaddeus Kosciuszko National Memorial

c/o Independence National Historical Park
313 Walnut Street
Philadelphia, PA 19106-2278
215-597-9618

This national memorial at Pine and Third Streets celebrates the life and accomplishments of Thaddeus Kosciuszko, the Polish-born patriot and hero of the Revolutionary War, and protects and interprets the modest, restored, red-brick townhouse where he rented a room during the winter of 1797-98. Kosciuszko is remembered for skillfully selecting and fortifying with artillery the strategic heights and redoubts above the Hudson River and river road, about 30 miles north of Albany, New York. At the age of 21, Kosciuszko's military engineering genius gave the American patriots the advantage of holding this strategically significant high ground, enabling them to win a stunning military victory against British forces, which led to the surrender of the British a few days later in October 1777 (see Saratoga National Historical Park entry). As a result, Kosciuszko was promoted to the distinguished rank of the Continental Army's chief engineer. The memorial, which is open daily, except Thanksgiving, Christmas, and New Year's Day, provides a few exhibits and a short slide program in English and in Polish. The site is a quarter-mile south of Independence National Historical Park on 3rd Street, at the corner of Pine Street.

Upper Delaware Scenic and Recreational River

R.R. 2, Box 2428
Beach Lake, PA 18405-9737
717-729-8251

This 75,000-acre (mostly privately owned) scenic and recreational river, along 73 miles of the free-flowing upper Delaware River in northeast Pennsylvania, is popular for rafting, boating, canoeing, kayaking, and tubing. Historic buildings, remains of a once-busy canal, the oldest existing wire suspension bridge in the United States, and the historic Zane Grey home and museum are among other highlights of this beautiful area. Canoe and boat rentals and campgrounds are located in the vicinity. Access is from New York Route 97.

Valley Forge National Historical Park

P.O. Box 953
Valley Forge, PA 19482-0953
610-783-1000

This 3,466-acre national historical park along the Schuylkill River in southeast Pennsylvania protects and interprets the Continental Army's encampment site during the brutally severe winter of 1777-78 during the Revolutionary War. General George Washington's Continental Army had been defeated at the Battle of Brandywine on September 11, opening the way for British troops to capture and occupy the city of Philadelphia. Washington's troops had failed to recapture the city with a surprise attack on the British in the Battle of Germantown on October 4. In mid-December, 12,000 discouraged, war-weary, ill-fed, scantily clothed, and poorly equipped American soldiers made their way onto the defensible, but wind-swept heights at Valley Forge.

The men immediately began building hundreds of log huts, in which they could seek shelter from the fury of the coming winter. Here on the gently rolling hills of Mount Joy and Mount Misery, the soldiers endured intense suffering and deprivation. In their crowded, damp, and freezing-cold quarters, most of the men had only tattered clothing, many had no shoes, and their food was usually a mixture of flour and water. While no battle was fought at Valley Forge, at least 2,000 men died from exposure, malnutrition, and disease, and at least 4,000 became unfit for military service.

The park contains Washington's headquarters, original earthworks, monuments and markers, and re-creations of log buildings and cannons. The visitor center provides interpretive exhibits, publications, and a small auditorium with an audiovisual program. Living history programs are presented from May to September. A self-guided interpretive drive, for which an audiotape tour is available at the visitor center, leads to key sites, including reconstructed huts, the Outer Line Defenses, the National Memorial Arch erected in 1917 to commemorate the "patience and fidelity" of the soldiers, and the two-story, stone Isaac Potts House that served as Washington's headquarters. A six-mile foot and bicycle path follows alongside much of the tour road, while on the north side of the river are a picnic area, ten miles of hiking trails, and the Schuylkill River Trail. The park is open daily, except Christmas. Access to the park from major highways (such as Exit 24 on the Pennsylvania Turnpike, I-276 from the east, and I-76 from the west) is well marked with signs to the visitor center at the junction of State Route 23 and Valley Forge Road.

RHODE ISLAND

Roger Williams National Memorial

282 North Main Street
Providence, RI 02903-1240
401-521-7266

This 4.5-acre national memorial commemorates the founding of the settlement "Providence Plantations" by Roger Williams (c. 1603–83), who promoted the ideal of a democratically governed colony that offered its residents religious freedom, tolerance, and the separation of church and state. Williams had been banished by the Puritan founders of the Massachusetts Bay Colony for his protests against civil laws that required church attendance, levied a tax in support of the government-sanctioned church, and denied non-church members the right to vote in political elections. He then moved south of Massachusetts, into the Narragansett Bay area, and by 1643 had established four settlements. In 1644 and 1663, Williams returned to England to obtain charters for these communities; these documents provided the legal foundation for the new colony of "Rhode Island and Providence Plantations" (the full name of the state of Rhode Island today).

A century after Roger Williams's death, the Bill of Rights of the U.S. Constitution guaranteed freedom of religion and separation of church and state. The national memorial, therefore, also commemorates his contribution to the establishment of these fundamental principles in the United States. The visitor center at the corner of North Main and Smith streets provides interpretive exhibits, audiovisual programs, and publications. It is open daily, except Thanksgiving, Christmas, and New Year's Day. The memorial is down the hill from the Rhode Island State House, at the corner of North Main and Smith streets.

VERMONT

Marsh-Billings-Rockefeller National Historical Park

Mailing address:
c/o National Park Service
99 Warren Street
Brookline, MA 02146
617-566-1689

This 643-acre national historical park at Woodstock in east-central Vermont commemorates the history of conservation and the principles of sound land stewardship and forestry. The park encompasses managed woodlands and pastures, manicured flower gardens and lawns, and the 26-room, Queen Anne-style "summer cottage" that was the home of two pioneer conservationists, George Perkins Marsh (1801–82) and Frederick Billings (1823–90).

Marsh, an attorney and diplomat who served in Turkey and Italy, wrote the landmark environmental-protection book, *Man and Nature*, published in 1864. In it, he expressed the fundamental conservation ethic that humans will ultimately face destruction unless they use natural resources wisely. Billings, who was president of the Northern Pacific Railroad,

was so deeply influenced by Marsh's book that he purchased his mentor's home, helped preserve his library, and became a leader in forest conservation in a period when Vermont's forested hills and mountains were being denuded by the potash industry and sheep farming. On this property, he planted thousands of trees, beginning what has become one of the oldest, continuously managed forests in America.

In the 1950s, Billings's granddaughter, Mary French Rockefeller, and her husband, Laurence S. Rockefeller, inherited the estate. Following Mrs. Rockefeller's death in 1997, Mr. Rockefeller generously donated the property to the nation as the Marsh-Billings National Historical Park. Over the years, his generosity also brought about the establishment or expansion of other national parks, including Virgin Islands and Grand Teton. His father, John D. Rockefeller, Jr., donated much of the land that lies within Acadia National Park.

The visitor center is currently located at the Billings Farm and Museum, a 350-acre dairy farm operated by the Woodstock Foundation. Hiking and horseback riding trails are available, and in winter, some of these routes are groomed for cross-country skiing. The mansion and grounds are open daily through the summer and early autumn. Tours of the garden and of the mansion, focusing on the art collection, are offered at $5 per tour. Access to the visitor center from Woodstock is just north on State Route 12.

VIRGINIA

Appomattox Court House National Historical Park

P.O. Box 218
Appomattox, VA 24522-0218
804-352-8987

This 1,775-acre national historical park, at the village of Appomattox Court House in central Virginia, protects and interprets the Civil War site where Confederate Gen. Robert E. Lee surrendered his 35,000-man Army of Northern Virginia to Union Gen.Ulysses S. Grant on April 9, 1865. It

91

was there also that Confederate weapons were surrendered, on April 12—four years to the day after the war began.

The visitor center in the reconstructed county court house provides interpretive exhibits, audiovisual programs, and publications. Living history programs are presented during the summer, and a walking tour of the reconstructed buildings is offered. The park is open daily, except national holidays. Access is by way of the Appomattox exit of U.S. Route 460 (about 20 miles east of Lynchburg), and just north on State Route 24.

Arlington House, The Robert E. Lee Memorial

Mailing address:
c/o George Washington Memorial
Parkway
Turkey Run Park
McLean, VA 22101-0001
703-557-0613

This 28-acre memorial, located in Arlington, Virginia, protects and interprets the elegant antebellum home known as Arlington House, which was completed in 1817 and owned by the Custis and Lee families. Robert E. Lee lived in this house for 30 years, before the outbreak of the Civil War. On April 17, 1861, Virginia seceded from the Union; on April 20, Lee resigned from the U.S. Army; on April 22, he was appointed commander of the state's military forces; and in May, Virginia and Lee's forces joined the Confederacy. On April 1865, the war ended when Lee surrendered his army's weapons to Union commander, Ulysses S. Grant, at Appomattox Court House in Virginia. In 1955, Arlington House was designated as a memorial to Robert E. Lee, a man who had gained respect of Americans in both the North and South.

Visitors touring Arlington House enter by the impressive marbled-columned, front portico and continue through rooms on the first and second floors. The house, which is located adjacent to Arlington National Cemetery, is open daily except Christmas and New Year's Day. Access from Washington, D.C., is a short walk or drive across the Potomac River by way of the Arlington Memorial Bridge, to the Arlington Memorial Cemetery visitor center

parking area, and a short walk up the hill to the mansion. From within Virginia, the area is reached by the George Washington Memorial Parkway. A shuttle service and the Metro subway's Blue Line stop at Arlington Cemetery.

Booker T. Washington National Monument

12130 B. T. Washington Highway
Hardy, VA 24101-9688
703-721-2094

This 224-acre national monument in the southern Virginia piedmont honors the life and accomplishments of Booker T. Washington (1856–1915), who rose from humble beginnings as a slave to be known ultimately as America's leading black educator. The monument protects and interprets the historic James Burroughs tobacco farm, where Washington was born and spent his childhood. At age 23, he became a teacher at the Hampton Institute, from which he graduated with honors. Two years later, he was named the principal of Tuskegee Institute in Tuskegee, Alabama.

The visitor center provides interpretive exhibits, an audiovisual program, and publications. The Plantation Trail leads visitors to a number of reconstructed farm buildings, and a picnic area is available. The monument is open daily, except Thanksgiving, Christmas, and New Year's Day. Access from I-81 is by way of I-581 through Roanoke to U.S. Route 220, then south 16 miles to Rocky Mount, and north through Burnt Chimney on State Route 122 to the monument entrance.

Colonial National Historical Park

P.O. Box 210
Yorktown, VA 23690-0210
804-898-3400

This 9,352-acre park in the Tidewater area of eastern Virginia protects and interprets two sites: part of the site of Jamestown, the first permanent English settlement in North America, founded in 1607 on Jamestown Island in the James River; and the site of the decisive American-French victory over British forces in 1781 in the Battle of Yorktown at the mouth of the York River. The two park units are connected by the 23-mile Colonial Parkway.

Jamestown

Hardships beset the budding community from the outset. A fever that was likely typhoid claimed many lives; the island's brackish water was undrinkable; perishable food spoiled; oppressively humid heat of the "sickly season" was virtually unbearable; prolific mosquitoes and other insects made life miserable; and in the first cold, damp winter, more than 60 settlers perished from illness and starvation. Two winters later, the death toll reached 500, leaving a mere 60; but in 1610, a large group of new settlers arrived from England just in time to save Jamestown from almost certain abandonment. From the beginning, there had been almost constant conflict between the settlers and the native Indians, who were alarmed by the rapid takeover of their traditional lands, especially with the settlers' clearing of land on which to grow tobacco. In 1622, the Powhatan Indians finally retaliated: close to 350 settlers were killed (about one-third of the population), and nearly all outlying settlements were destroyed.

Over the next several years, as newcomers arrived, the colonists came close to wiping out the Indian tribes in the surrounding area as new settlements, villages, farms, and tobacco plantations sprang up farther inland. By 1650, Jamestown was no longer the military and commercial center of the colony, but remained only the seat of colonial government. Finally, some colonists outraged over the strict policies of the English Crown's colonial governor staged a rebellion and, in 1676, burned Jamestown to the ground. Governmental buildings were quickly rebuilt, but when the legislative building again burned down in 1698, the colonial capital was moved inland to Middle Plantation, renamed Williamsburg.

Today, the eastern part of the original Jamestown settlement lies within the Jamestown unit of Colonial National Historical Park. Adjacent to the park is the affiliated, 22-acre Jamestown National Historic Site, containing the western part of the settlement, along with ruins of the 17th-century Jamestown church tower and the statue of the Powhatan Indian, Pocahontas. This site is owned and managed by the Association for the Preservation of Virginia Antiquities, a private nonprofit organization. Also adjacent to the park is Jamestown Settlement, run by the Jamestown-Yorktown Foundation, a quasi-governmental agency of the Commonwealth of Virginia. This area features recreations of James Fort and a Powhatan Indian village; replicas of three square-rigged sailing ships like those that carried Jamestown's founding settlers from England to Virginia; and a museum complex on Jamestown and the Powhatan Indians.

Yorktown

In September 1781, while the Continental Army's Gen. George Washington succeeded in leading the British forces into believing he was poised to attack them at New York City, he organized 2,000 American and 5,000 French soldiers for rapid deployment south to Virginia. This strategic shift of manpower was carried out in anticipation of launching an attack upon the British naval base at Yorktown, where one-third of all British troops in America were stationed. Washington's troops were reinforced by 4,000 Continental soldiers already in Virginia, plus 3,000 Virginia militiamen. At about the same time, a large battle fleet of French warships arrived in Chesapeake Bay off the Virginia coast and attacked a British fleet, causing extensive damage and forcing it to sail back to New York for repairs. The French fleet then formed a blockade across the mouth of Chesapeake Bay and the York River.

On October 9, Washington's allied army launched its artillery attack of British-held Yorktown. After nine days of nonstop bombardment, with British supplies dwindling and no hope that their navy could break through the blockade and rescue them, British commander Lord Charles Cornwallis requested a ceasefire on October 17 to discuss the terms of surrender. Two days later, the defeated British army yielded up its arms as they marched by the victors. This historic surrender signaled the final major military engagement in the Revolutionary War.

The national historical park has two visitor centers—one focusing on the Yorktown unit, the other on Jamestown. Both centers provide interpretive exhibits, programs, and publications. Self-guided and interpreter-guided tours are offered, as well as driving tours with interpretive stops at points of interest. Access to the park is by way of U.S. Route 17 from I-95 near Fredericksburg; by way of I-64 southeast from Richmond or northwest from Norfolk; or by State Route 5 from Richmond, a route that passes a number of historic plantations along the north shore of the James River.

Fredericksburg and Spotsylvania County Battlefields Memorial National Military Park

120 Chatham Lane
Fredericksburg, VA 22405-2508
540-371-0802

This 7,787-acre national military park, comprising numerous scattered units in and near Fredericksburg, protects and interprets four major Civil War battles: Fredericksburg, December 11–13, 1862; Chancellorsville, May 1–4, 1863; the Wilderness, May 5–6, 1864; and Spotsylvania Court House, May 8–21, 1864. The park also features Chatham Manor, Old Salem Church, and the building in which Confederate Gen. Stonewall Jackson died.

Fredericksburg

Following a number of intense clashes between Union and Confederate troops at Fredericksburg in December 1862, one of the worst military disasters of the Civil War resulted in a devastating defeat for the Union army, with casualties totaling at least 12,500 men. The site of this killing field was below Marye's Heights, a strategic hill that, as was known to the Union forces, was bristling with Confederate batteries of cannon and infantry. What the Union commanders did not know, however, was what lay hidden at the base of the hill, along a sunken road and out of sight behind the breastwork of a stone wall.

As the first Union brigade of soldiers charged across a 400-yard expanse of open ground in an attempt to storm the hill, they were suddenly mowed down by the massive volley of Confederate musket fire that erupted from behind the wall. From noon until dark, wave after wave charged across the field, but each suffered the same fate. The slaughter continued, with not a single Northerner ever reaching the wall. Reeling from this defeat, the demoralized Union army withdrew northward across the Rappahannock River.

Chancellorsville

Nearly five months later, in early May 1863,

the next fierce battle occurred around Chancellorsville, about ten miles to the northwest of Fredericksburg. Even though the Confederates were greatly outnumbered, they nevertheless achieved another victory. In the final clash of the battle, Confederates opened a withering attack upon a 22,000-man Union force that, earlier in the day, had captured the defenses in and around Fredericksburg. Heavy casualties from those several days of fighting totaled more than 17,000 Union and nearly 13,000 Confederate soldiers.

The Wilderness

A year later, two days of savage, confused, hand-to-hand combat occurred between Union and Confederate armies in an area of dense scrubby pines and oaks known as the Wilderness, about 15 miles northwest of Fredericksburg. The smoke from forest fires reduced visibility further, adding to the chaos of the conflict. Union casualties totaled nearly 18,000 men, while the Confederates sustained more than 8,000 killed, wounded, or captured. Unlike previous Union commanders in the Virginia campaign, Lt. Gen. Ulysses S. Grant refused to retreat. Instead, he ordered his forces on southward, in a campaign designed to wear down and ultimately defeat Gen. Robert E. Lee's Confederate army.

Spotsylvania Court House

Several days later, the armies clashed again in fierce combat at the important crossroads junction of Spotsylvania Court House. Some of the most brutal combat of the Civil War occurred at a U-shaped salient known as the "mule shoe." The Union forces far outnumbered and soon overwhelmed the Confederates. As more and more reinforcements on both sides poured into the battle around the jutting angle, savage hand-to-hand warfare erupted, with soldiers using bayonets, knives, clubs, rocks, and bare fists. For 20 hours, the slaughtering raged on, made worse by a downpour of rain and deepening mud, and after midnight, the Southerners finally retreated to form new defense lines. For all the fighting, which continued for the next two weeks, there were no measurable gains for either side. Following the battles of the Wilderness and Spotsylvania Court House, the area around Fredericksburg became an enormous open-air hospital, where surgeons labored around the clock attending to the 20,000 wounded Union and Confederate soldiers.

The park has two visitor centers, providing interpretive exhibits, an audiovisual program, and publications. One is near the base of Marye's Heights at 1013 Lafayette Boulevard in the Fredericksburg unit, and the other is at Chancellorsville, eight miles west of I-95 on State Route 3. A self-guided auto tour and self-guided walking routes lead to points of interest. Other interpretive facilities include exhibit shelters at the Wilderness and Spotsylvania Court House units. The park headquarters is located in the red-brick, 18th-century, Georgian-style plantation mansion, Chatham Manor, to the north of the Rappahannock River from Fredericksburg. This grand old structure served as a Union army headquarters and field hospital during the Civil War. The park also offers walking tours and living-history talks during the summer months, and picnic areas are available at all four battlefield units, Chatham Manor, and the Stonewall Jackson Shrine. Access to the park includes State Route 3, east from I-95 to Fredericksburg and west from I-95 to the Chancellorsville and Wilderness units. One of the accesses to the Spotsylvania Court House unit is on State Route 613, southeast from State Route 3, just to the east of the Wilderness Battlefield.

George Washington Birthplace National Monument

R.R. 1, Box 717
Washington's Birthplace, VA 22443-9688
804-224-1732

This 550-acre national monument on the banks of Popes Creek, a tributary of the Potomac River, in tidewater Virginia protects and interprets the 18th-century tobacco plantation manor house in which George Washington, the celebrated Revolutionary War general and first president of the United States, was born on February 22, 1732. In addition to the mansion that was Washington's childhood home, the monument includes landscaped gardens and several generations of Washington family tombs. The monument provides interpretive exhibits, programs, and tours. Self-guided nature walks and trails lead through the prop-

erty. The National Park Service cautions visitors to be alert for ticks. The monument is open daily, except Christmas and New Year's Day. Access from I-95 is by way of State Route 3, 38 miles east of Fredericksburg.

George Washington Memorial Parkway

Mailing address:
Turkey Run Park
McLean, VA 22101-0001
703-289-2530

This 7,247-acre memorial parkway, running from George Washington's home at Mount Vernon to just below the Great Falls of the Potomac River protects the natural scenery along the river as a memorial to the celebrated Revolutionary War general and first president of the United States. Numerous places of historic interest and natural beauty lie along the route. From south to north, they include Fort Hunt, where batteries guarded the river approach from 1898 to 1918; Dyke Marsh, a habitat for birds such as herons, egrets, rails, and ducks; Daingerfield Island, an area with hiking paths, recreational facilities, and the Washington Sailing Marina; Roaches Run Waterfowl Sanctuary, a popular birdwatching area; Gravelly Point, a spot that offers an excellent view across the river to the nation's capital; access to Columbia Island, on which are located the Lyndon Baines Johnson Memorial Grove, the Navy and Marine Memorial, and the Columbia Island Marina; parking for the pedestrian bridge to Theodore Roosevelt Island; and Turkey Run Park, an area affording views of the palisades of the Potomac.

Maggie L. Walker National Historic Site

Mailing address:
c/o Richmond National Battlefield Park
3215 East Broad Street
Richmond, VA 23223-7517
804-780-1380

This one-acre national historic site, at 110 East Leigh Street, in Richmond, honors the memory and accomplishments of Maggie L. Walker, a former slave's daughter who established in 1903 one of the first African-American banks in the United States, became the first American woman to serve as president of a bank, and was a prominent leader of Richmond's black community. The site protects and interprets the Maggie L. Walker House, a restored, red-brick townhouse containing original Walker furnishings. Guided tours are offered, and interpretive exhibits and a video are presented. The site is open on Wednesdays through Sundays, except Thanksgiving, Christmas, and New Year's Day. Access from I-95 is by way of Exit 76A or 76B and then following signs to Leigh Street.

Manassas National Battlefield Park

12521 Lee Highway
Manassas, VA 22110-2005
703-754-1861

This 5,071-acre national battlefield park, about 25 miles southwest of Washington, D.C., protects and interprets the site of the Civil War's Battles of First and Second Manassas, on July 21, 1861, and August 28–30, 1862, respectively. Both conflicts were won by Confederate forces and marked the height of Confederate power during the war.

The Battle of First Manassas
In the Battle of First Manassas (also known as the Battle of Bull Run), the first real clash of the Civil War, the Southerners adopted a strong defensive strategy. Troops were massed along the south bank of the meandering course of Bull Creek to protect the strategically important Manassas Junction where two railroad lines met and to block a Union army advance toward Richmond, the capital of the Confederacy. The Southerners were initially forced to retreat. But costly Union errors in the vicinity of Henry Hill and the arrival of trainloads of Confederate reinforcements suddenly turned what had appeared a victory for the Northerners into confused disarray and a humiliating retreat back to Washington. Casualties totaled nearly 3,000 Union and around 2,000 Confederate soldiers.

The Battle of Second Manassas
The Battle of Second Manassas, just over 13 months later, began with a classic military maneuver, in which Confederate forces made a 56-mile swing around and behind Union troop positions, capturing and destroying their sup-

ply depot at Manassas Junction and severing the communications and supply lines to Washington. The Northerners retaliated, attempting to triumph before Confederate reinforcements could arrive, but after achieving a couple of successes, the overconfident Union commander assumed that the Southerners were withdrawing and ordered his troops forward in a major assault. Suddenly, fresh Confederate reinforcements unleashed a massive firestorm, and a half-hour later, the surviving Union army was forced to retreat. A wave of 30,000 Confederates then charged in a powerful, double-barreled counterattack. After this ferocious combat, the badly battered Union army, which had come close to being annihilated, trudged back to the protective defenses around Washington. Casualties in this battle totaled about 14,000 Union and nearly 8,500 Confederate soldiers.

Today, a visitor center at Henry Hill provides interpretive exhibits, audiovisual programs, and publications, and an interpretive facility on Stuart's Hill provides interpretation during the summer. A mile-long, self-guided interpretive trail leads visitors from the center to a number of key points. A 1.4-mile loop trail runs along Bull Run. A 12-mile driving tour offers a more extensive, interpretive view of the Second Manassas battlefield. In addition to numerous hiking trails, the park maintains an extensive network of equestrian trails. A picnic area is available near the "Dogan Ridge" interpretive stop, off State Route 234, north of U.S. Route 29. The park is open daily, except Christmas. The National Park Service cautions visitors to be careful when crossing, entering, or leaving any of the public highways that pass through the park. Access from Washington, D.C., is southwest 26 miles on I-66 to Exit 47 and north a half-mile on State Route 234 to the visitor center.

Petersburg National Battlefield

1539 Hickory Hill Road
Petersburg, VA 23803-4721
804-732-3531

This 2,744-acre, five-unit national battlefield in southern Virginia protects and interprets several Civil War sites relating to the Union army's nearly ten-month campaign from June

19, 1864, to April 2, 1865, to seize the Confederates' key railroad center at Petersburg and cut their supply lines. The Union army maintained relentless daily pressure of mortar shelling, small arms fire, and skirmishing, and by February 1865, 110,000 well-supplied Union troops were pressing against Petersburg and its 60,000 hungry and cold Confederate soldiers.

By March, Confederate forces made two attempts to break out. One resulted in the short-lived capture of a Union fort, and the other failed to prevent Union forces from severing the last supply railroad line into Petersburg. On April 2, the Northerners launched a final, massive bombardment of Petersburg. That night, the Confederate military fled the city at the same time that Richmond, the capital of the Confederacy, was being evacuated. It was only a week away from the surrender of the Confederate army at Appomattox Court House.

Today, the visitor center in the national battlefield's main unit provides interpretive exhibits, an audiovisual program, and publications. A four-mile tour drive leads from the center, with interpretive stops at places such as two Confederate batteries captured by African-American soldiers; Fort Stedman, which was briefly captured by Confederate soldiers in a desperate effort to break out of the siege; and the huge crater that resulted from a powerful Union explosion detonated beneath a Confederate fortification.

Other units of the battlefield are linked by a 16-mile tour drive, highlighting a number of Union and Confederate forts and the place where the Northerners succeeded in severing the last major supply line into Petersburg. Eight miles to the northeast of Petersburg, in the city of Hopewell, is the City Point unit of the park including the building that served as Union Gen. Ulysses S. Grant's command center.

In the summer, living history programs are presented in the park. Hiking and bicycling trails, and picnic facilities are available. The national battlefield is open daily, except on winter holidays. Access to both the main park unit and City Point is by way of U.S. Route 36. The Five Forks unit is reached from I-85 at Exit 53, following the signs through Dinwiddie and proceeding north five miles on Dinwiddie Courthouse Road (State Route 627).

Prince William Forest Park

18100 Park Headquarters Road
Triangle, VA 22172-0209
703-221-7181

This 18,571-acre park, about 30 miles south of Washington, D.C., protects an ecologically rich area of predominantly deciduous forest, containing springs, creeks, and waterfalls of the Quantico Creek watershed. The park was established by President Franklin D. Roosevelt to give urban youth groups an opportunity to attend summer camps, where they could enjoy the benefits of the outdoors. The camps and other structures were built by the Civilian Conservation Corps as part of the nation's program to help get people back to work after the Great Depression of the 1930s.

Among the many species of trees in the park are Virginia pine, eastern hemlock, tulip tree (yellow poplar), sassafras, American sycamore, sweetgum, beech, oaks (white, post, chestnut, red, black, and blackjack), river birch, eastern redbud, flowering dogwood, and red maple. Mammals include whitetail deer, red and gray foxes, beaver, raccoon, opossum, and gray squirrels. Of the numerous birds, there are wild turkey, barred owl, woodpeckers (pileated, red-bellied, and downy), blue jay, Carolina chickadee, tufted titmouse, white-breasted nuthatch, Carolina wren, wood thrush, warblers (yellow, yellow-rumped, pine, prairie, black-and-white, worm-eating, Kentucky, and hooded), American redstart, common yellowthroat, ovenbird, Louisiana waterthrush, yellow-breasted chat, Baltimore oriole, scarlet tanager, cardinal, rufous-sided towhee, and white-throated and song sparrows.

A scenic drive and nearly 40 miles of hiking trails wind through the park. A visitor center, open daily except Christmas, provides interpretive exhibits and programs on the area's human and natural history. Picnic areas and campgrounds are available. Primitive camping is permitted in the Chopawamsic Backcountry Area. Access to the park is by way of I-95; take Exit 150B and drive west a quarter-mile on State Route 619. Alternatively, drive 22 miles north of Fredericksburg on I-95 to Exit 150B and go west on State Route 619.

Richmond National Battlefield Park

3215 East Broad Street
Richmond, VA 23223-7517
804-226-1981

This 820-acre, 11-unit national battlefield park protects and interprets 13 engagements during the Civil War in which the Union army sought to capture the capital of the Confederacy. The Peninsular (or Peninsula) Campaign, from mid-March to early July 1862, was continually hampered by a prolonged period of heavy rains, overflowing creeks and rivers, washed-out bridges, and muddy ground. It culminated in a series of brutal and bloody engagements of the Seven Days' Battles and ended indecisively. Casualties totaled nearly 16,000 Union soldiers and more than 22,000 Confederates.

Nearly two years later, the Virginia Campaign included the brief but horrendous slaughter on June 3, 1864, in the Battle of Cold Harbor, eight miles to the northeast of Richmond, and ended with the Union army's capture of Petersburg and Richmond on April 2, 1865. The park interprets the Cold Harbor battle site, where nearly 6,000 Union soldiers were killed or wounded in a single hour, as Confederate troops suddenly rose into view from behind a massive earthworks and launched a flaming attack from their massed artillery and muskets.

The visitor center, at 3215 East Broad Street, Richmond, provides interpretive exhibits, audiovisual programs, and publications. The center is at the site of one of the Confederacy's most extensive hospital complexes, Chimborazo General, which served more than 75,000 sick and wounded soldiers. Other interpretive facilities include the Cold Harbor visitor contact station just off State Route 156 to the northeast of Richmond and the Fort Harrison orientation center, which is open seasonally, on Battlefield Park Road off State Route 5 between Richmond and the I-295 interchange. Short interpretive trails are offered at Chickahominy Bluffs, Cold Harbor, Gaines' Mill, Malvern Hill, Fort Harrison, Fort Brady, and Drewry's Bluff units. The ten park units and visitor center are linked by an 80-mile drive, mostly on U.S. and state highways. A self-guided audiotape tour is available at the visitor center. The battlefield units are open daily, and the visitor center is open daily, except Thanksgiving, Christmas, and New Year's Day. Access to the visitor center from I-95 southbound is by way of Exit 74B onto Franklin Street, then right onto 14th Street and right onto Broad Street. From I-95 northbound, take Exit 74C onto 17th Street southbound and turn left onto Broad Street.

Wolf Trap Farm Park for the Performing Arts

1551 Trap Road
Vienna, VA 22182-1643
703-255-1800

This 130-acre park about eight miles from Washington, D.C., was established as a gift from Catherine Filene Shouse to "people of all ages in all walks of life to enjoy the performing arts in a natural setting of woods, fields, and stream." The park, which is open daily except Christmas, is an open-air pavilion that accommodates an audience of nearly 7,000 in the pavilion and on the lawn. The park is a partnership between the National Park Service, which manages the park and provides interpretive programs and backstage tours, and the Wolf Trap Foundation for the Performing Arts, which arranges schedules for Filene Center's summer performances and festivals. During July and August, the Park Service also sponsors workshops and performances for children at the Theatre-in-the-Woods. For information on the latter, call 703-255-1827.

Access to the park from the Capital Beltway (I-495) southbound is at Exit 11B (Tyson's Corner/Route 123), proceeding a short way on State Route 123, then westbound on State Route 7, left onto Towlston Road, and continuing a mile to the entrance. For visitors attending Filene Center performances, access is also by way of the Dulles Toll Road and its Wolf Trap exit, up to two hours prior to the start of events. Tickets are required for most performances. Program information: Wolf Trap Foundation for the Performing Arts, 1624 Trap Rd., Vienna, VA 22182; 703-255-1900 or 703-255-1860.

Bluestone National Scenic River

c/o New River Gorge National River
P.O. Box 246
Glen Jean, WV 25846-0246
304-465-0508

This 4,309-acre national scenic river in southern West Virginia protects 11 miles of this free-flowing river amid the ruggedly spectacular Bluestone Gorge and a richly forested area of the Appalachian Plateau. Activities include birdwatching, fishing, canoeing and rafting during periods of high water, hiking on eight-mile Bluestone Trail through the gorge, and public hunting in all but the upper 3.5 miles of the national scenic river during the designated season. Visitor facilities, such as picnic areas, campgrounds, meals, and lodging, are available in Bluestone and Pipestem state parks at each end of the national scenic river. Access is by way of State Route 20, between New River Gorge National River and I-77.

Gauley River National Recreation Area

c/o New River Gorge National River
P.O. Box 246
Glen Jean, WV 25846-0246
304-465-0508

This 11,145-acre national recreation area in south-central West Virginia protects 25 miles of the free-flowing Gauley River and six miles of the Meadow River, where they pass through beautiful gorges and forested valleys. The Gauley, containing several Class V+ rapids, is ranked as one of the most exciting whitewater rafting rivers in the eastern United States. Other activities include hiking, birdwatching, and fishing. Access is from the surrounding highways: U.S. Routes 60 and 19 and State Routes 39 and 16.

Harpers Ferry National Historical Park

P.O. Box 65
Harpers Ferry, WV 25425-0065
304-535-6298

This 2,287-acre national historical park at the confluence of the Shenandoah and Potomac rivers protects and interprets a number of themes that run through Harpers Ferry's history. Transportation links, including the Chesapeake & Ohio Canal and the Baltimore & Ohio Railroad, both begun in 1828, were extended westward through this strategic gap in the mountains. Factories and mills were established here, along with a federal armory and arsenal, which increased its annual production of firearms from 10,000 rifles and muskets in 1810 to more than 600,000 rifles, muskets, and pistols in 1860. Abolitionist John Brown and 20 supporters seized the federal armory in 1859 in an unsuccessful attempt to obtain 100,000 rifles and muskets with which to free slaves in the South.

During the Civil War, Harpers Ferry's strategic location on key railroad routes and between the North and South led to the destruction of its armory, factories, mills, and railroad bridges. The setting for this park is the magnificent landscape of rivers and richly forested mountains that President Thomas Jefferson characterized as "perhaps one of the most stupendous scenes in Nature." And also during the Civil War, Harpers Ferry became one of a number of Union garrison towns in which runaway slaves sought a safe haven. In 1864, a school was started to help educate former slaves, and in 1867, two years after the end of the war, Storer Normal School (subsequently Storer College) was founded there.

The visitor center, located just off U.S. Route 340, provides interpretive exhibits, an audiovisual program, and publications. Shuttle-bus service takes visitors from the center to the Lower Town District. Among the highlights of the park are the restored buildings of Lower Town, including Harper House, the town's oldest structure. An interpreter-led tour from spring through autumn includes the ruins of the 19th-century industrial center, the old federal armory buildings that have been restored for use by Storer College, and Bolivar Heights. Scenic hikes are also available on the Appalachian Trail along the Virginia side of the Shenandoah River and up to Maryland Heights across the Potomac from Harpers Ferry. Access to the park is by way of U.S. Route 340, between Frederick, Maryland, and Charles Town, West Virginia.

New River Gorge National River

P.O. Box 246
Glen Jean, WV 25846-0246
304-465-0508

This 70,911-acre national river in southern West Virginia protects 53 miles of the magnificently scenic New River between Hinton and Fayetteville where it flows through richly forested country and a spectacular gorge that rises more than 800 feet above the rapids-filled river. The New River is ranked as one of the best whitewater rivers in the eastern United States for rafting and kayaking. Other activities include hiking and horseback riding on the many miles of trails, along with birdwatching, fishing, and public hunting during the designated season. There are several visitor centers, including one located at the north end of the 3,030-foot-long New River Gorge Bridge on U.S. Route 19. A campground, meals, and cabins are available in Babcock State Park, which is within the national river boundaries just off State Route 41. Access to the river is by way of three highways that cut through the area: U.S. Route 19, State Route 41, and I-64. Amtrak service is provided to Hinton and Prince, with a flag stop at Thurmond.

Friends of the Parks Organizations

Appalachian Mountain Club
(Appalachian National Scenic Trail)
65 Woodland Street
Sherborn, MA 01770
508-653-2602

Appalachian Trail Conference
P.O. Box 807
Harpers Ferry, WV 25425
304- 535-6331

Assateague Coastal Trust
P.O. Box 731
Berlin, MD 21811
410- 629-1538

Association for the Preservation of Cape Cod
P.O. Box 636
Orleans, MA 02653
508-255-4142

Billings Farm Museum/Woodstock Foundation, Inc.
(Marsh-Billings-Rockefeller National Historical Park)
P.O. Box 489
Woodstock, VT 05091
802-457-2355

C & O Canal Association
P.O. Box 366
Glen Echo, MD 20812
301-983-0825

Eleanor Roosevelt Center at Val-Kill, Inc.
P.O. Box 255
Hyde Park, NY 12538
914-229-5302

Elizabeth Cady Stanton Foundation
(Women's Rights National Historical Park)
P.O. Box 603
Seneca Falls, NY 12114
315-568-4238

Fire Island Lighthouse Preservation Society
4640 Captree Island
Captree Island, NY 11702
516-321-7028

Fort Stanwix Garrison
12 E. Park Street
Rome, NY 13440
315-336-2090

Frederick W. Vanderbilt Garden Association, Inc.
(Vanderbilt Mansion National Historic Site)
P.O. Box 239
Hyde Park, NY 12538
914-229-9115

Freedom Trail Foundation
Boston National Historical Park
Boston, MA 02129-4543
617-242-5695

Friendship Hill Association
P.O. Box 24
New Geneva, PA 15467
724-329-5512

Friends of Acadia
P.O. Box 725
Bar Harbor, ME 04609
207-288-3340

Friends of Battle Road, The
(Minuteman National Historical Park)
P.O. Box 95
Lincoln Center, MA 01973
617-944-3160

Friends of Big Hunting Creek
(Catoctin Mountain Park)
7003 Glen Court
Frederick, MD 21702
301-663-3966

Friends of Boston Harbor Islands, Inc.
23 Holbrook Street
Jamaica Plain, MA 02130
617-740-4290

Friends of Bull Run
(Manassas National Battlefield Park)
P.O. Box 402
The Plains, VA 22171
540-253-5501

Friends of Claude Moore Colonial Farm
(George Washington Memorial Parkway)
6310 Georgetown Pike
McLean, VA 22101
703-442-7557

Friends of Edison National Historic Site
342 Main Street
West Orange, NJ 07052
201-736-2916

Friends of Frederick Douglass
253 West Avenue
Rochester, NY 14611
716-325-7314

Friends of Gateway
72 Reade Street
New York, NY 10007
212-513-7555

Friends of Great Falls Tavern
(C & O Canal National Historical Park)
11725 Piney Meetinghouse Road
Potomac, MD 20854
301-983-1537

Friends of Independence
313 Walnut Street
Philadelphia, PA 19106
215-597-7919

Friends of Lindenwald
c/o Martin Van Buren National Historic Site
P.O. Box 545
Kinderhook, NY 02106
518-758-9869

Friends of Monocacy National Battlefield, Inc.
P.O. Box 4101
Frederick, MD 21705
301-694-1083

Friends of National Parks at Gettysburg
P.O. Box 3632
Gettysburg, PA 17325
717-334-0772

Friends of Prince William Forest Park
P.O. Box 209
Triangle, VA 22172
703-221-7181

Friends of Saratoga Battlefield
648 Route 32
Stillwater, NY 12170
518-664-9821

Friends of the Blackstone National Corridor
6 Valley Stream
Cumberland, RI 02864
401-334-2153

Friends of the Blue Ridge Parkway
P.O. Box 20986
Roanoke, VA 24018
704-687-8722

Friends of the Delaware Water Gap NRA
c/o Pocono Mountains Vacation Bureau
Stroudsburg, PA 18360
717-421-5791

Friends of the Statue of Liberty and Ellis Island, Inc.
17 Battery Park Place, 10th Floor
New York, NY 10004
212-425-5704

Friends of Valley Forge
P.O. Box 953
Valley Forge, PA 19481
610-640-9681

Friends of the William Floyd Estate
c/o Fire Island National Seashore
120 Laurel Street
Patchogue, NY 11772-3596
516-289-4810

Glen Echo Foundation, The
7300 MacArthur Boulevard
Glen Echo, MD 20812
301-320-2330

Heritage Partners, Inc.
(Boston Harbor Islands NRA)
65 Mt. Vernon Street
Boston, MA 02108
617-723-7122

Independence Hall Association
320 Chestnut Street
Philadelphia, PA 19106
215-925-7877

Lowell Regatta Festival Foundation
(Lowell National Historical Park)
P.O. Box 21
Lowell, MA 01853
508-454-7339

Potomac Conservancy, The
(C & O Canal National Historical Park)
4022 Hummer Road
Annandale, VA 22003
703-642-9880

Potomac Heritage Trail Association
5229 Benson Avenue
Baltimore, MD 21227

Quincy Partnership
(Adams National Historic Site)
P.O. Box 488
Quincy, MA 02170
617-773-3551

Rough Riders/Theodore Roosevelt
Inaugural Site Foundation
641 Delaware Avenue
Buffalo, NY 14202
716-884-0096

Salem Partnership
(Salem Maritime National Historic Site)
6 Central Street
Salem, MA 01970
508-741-8100

Save Historic Antietam Foundation, Inc.
P.O. Box 550
Sharpsburg, MD 21782
301-791-7880

Statue of Liberty-Ellis Island Foundation, Inc.
52 Vanderbilt Avenue, 4th Floor
New York, NY 10017
212-883-1986

Theodore Roosevelt Association
(Sagamore Hill National Historic Site)
P.O. Box 719
Oyster Bay, NY 11771
516-291-6319

Cooperating Associations

Civil War Trust
1225 I Street, NW
Washington, DC 20005
202-326-8420

Eastern National Park & Monument Association
446 N. Lane
Conshohocken, PA 19428
610-832-0555

George Washington Birthplace National Memorial Association.
1730 Pope's Creek Road
Washington's Birthplace, VA 22443
804-224-7895

Harpers Ferry Historical Association
P.O. Box 197
Harpers Ferry, WV 25425
304-535-6881

Historic Hampton, Inc.
c/o Hampton National Historic Site
535 Hampton Lane
Towson, MD 21286
410-962-0688

National Trust for Historic Preservation
1785 Massachusetts Avenue, N.W.
Washington, DC 20036
202-673-4000

Pocono Environmental Education Center
(Delaware Water Gap NRA)
Road 2, Box 1010
Dingmans Ferry, PA 18328
717-828-2319

Roosevelt Vanderbilt Historical Association
P.O. Box 235
Hyde Park, NY 1238
914-229-9300

Shenandoah Natural History Association
3655 U.S. Highway 211 East
Luray, VA 22835
540-999-3581

Steamtown Volunteer Association
c/o Steamtown National Historic Site
150 S. Washington Avenue
Scranton, PA 18503
717-346-0660

Student Conservation Association
1800 N. Kent Street
Arlington, VA 22209
703-524-2441

Valley Forge Park Interpretive Association
c/o Valley Forge National Historical Park
P.O. Box 953
Valley Forge, PA 19482
610-783-1074

Weir Farm Heritage Trust
735 Nod Hill Road
Wilton, CT 06897
203-761-9945

LOCAL COLOR

The Wildlife

"Texas" means friend.

Texas was a country before it was a state.

25 languages.

65 nationalities.

Texans believe life is too important to be dull.

The Wildflowers

The state flower is the Bluebonnet.

Over 5,000 species of wildflowers.

There's even a Wildflower Center (Thanks to Lady Bird Johnson).

Texas does not have blue grass. It just seems that way.

It's like a whole other country.®

Even the vacations are bigger in Texas. From the yarn-spinning charm of our native citizenry to hills carpeted with our native flowers, you'll find it all in Texas. It's more than you think. It's like a whole other country. For your free Texas travel guide, you can visit our web site at 💻 **www.TravelTex.com** or call us at ☎ **1-800-8888-TEX (Ext. 1290).** So give us a call, y'all.

NPCA Checks
Save Our Parks!

Every order helps preserve our country's most precious areas. Every time you order, royalties go directly to the National Parks and Conservation Association.

Return Address Labels - six scenes match your checks!

Hemp Checkbook Cover features the NPCA logo

Cotton Covers- select your favorite scene

Acadia

Everglades

Yellowstone

Arches

Smoky Mountains

Yosemite

autiful rotating ries features e Great Smoky ountains, Yosemite, ches, Yellowstone, adia, and Everglades tional Parks.

N A T I O N A L   P A R K S   C H E C K S   O R D E R   F O R M

eck Your Choice Below:	200 Singles	150 Duplicates	Total
National Parks Check Series (6 designs) (NP)	❏ $15.95	❏ $17.95	$_____
240 National Parks Labels (6 designs) (NP-LB)	....	Add $12.95	$_____

eckbook Covers:

Hemp Logo Cover (HNP-UQLO)......................................Add $14.95		$_____
Cotton Cover (CNP -UQLO)...Add $11.95		$_____

Select Scene: ❏ Acadia ❏ Everglades ❏ Yellowstone
❏ Arches ❏ Smoky Mountains ❏ Yosemite

SUBTOTAL $_____
Add 6.5% tax for Minnesota residents only $_____
Delivery ❏ $1.95 per item OR PRIORITY ❏ $3.95 per item $_____
TOTAL ENCLOSED: $_____
GD

ayment type
❏ Check enclosed–make payable to: Message!Products™ No COD's
❏ Debit my checking account (CHECK ORDERS ONLY) Signature_____
❏ Charge to: ❏ Visa ❏ Mastercard ❏ American Express ❏ Discover
t. No._____Exp. Date___/___ Signature_____

IMPORTANT! Include the following with this form:
❏ Voided check indicating a starting number # _____ for your new order
  (If none given we will start your order at 101)
❏ Deposit ticket from the same account
❏ Three lines of personalization for matching labels: (see left side!)

_____
_____
_____

❏ Daytime Telephone Number:(_____)_____
  (CONFIDENTIAL - in case of questions about your order only)

Please allow 3-5 weeks processing & delivery OR 1-3 weeks for PRIORITY delivery

To order, send complete form to:
Message!Products   or fax to:
P.O. Box 64800   1-800-790-6684
St. Paul, MN   or order online!
55164-0800   www.messagecheck.com

QUESTIONS? 1-800-243-2565

IF WE DON'T PROTECT THEM, WHO WILL?

LEND YOUR VOICE TO HELP SAVE OUR CROWN JEWELS.

The national parks belong to you and me, and they are the most important, meaningful and irreplaceable resource we have to give to future generations.

Unfortunately, our parks are in crisis! Almost every single one of the 378 national park units is troubled by problems of overcrowding, pollution and destructive uses that threaten to permanently damage these precious places...but there is hope.

For 80 years the National Parks and Conservation Association has been the only private, non-profit citizens' organization dedicated solely to preserving and protecting our National Park System. Over the years, some of our accomplishments have included: saving parks from toxic mining plans and nearby nuclear waste dumps, brokering pollution-abating air quality agreements, and working with Congress to implement concessions reform — that stopped businesses from profiting unfairly from the parks!

Our work is far from over and we need your help now! Please join National Parks and Conservation Association and lend your voice to the nearly 400,000 others who help us in our daily fight to save these parks. Thank you!